Let's Talk ABOUT MONEY

The Girlfriends' Guide to Protecting Her ASSets

Let's Talk ABOUT MONEY

The Girlfriends' Guide to Protecting Her ASSets

JANICE GOLDMAN

MAURICE BASSETT

books for athletes of the mind

For my mother

I dedicate this book to my mother who, in 1956, took me to Devon Avenue on the north side of Chicago to Hornblower & Weeks, an old-fashioned brokerage firm where a ticker tape machine could be seen along the top of the wall. I honor this remarkable woman for introducing me to the arena of investments for women at a time when very few women showed much interest in finance.

Brava, Mom, for being a pioneer and for including me in that world so that it could become a possibility for me.

There are no mistakes in life. Everything we do and expose our children to matters. My mom, who was often referred to as the family idiot, was responsible for accumulating and maintaining the family wealth.

I honor, respect, and admire you, Mom. Thank you for your love, your strength, and for the exposure to possibilities.

Contents

Discussion 4: Let's Talk about Parents

Discussion 5: Let's Talk about Retirement

Foreword

As a former director with Women & Co., a division of Citigroup, I was introduced to Janice Goldman through our training and development program. Surrounded by men in a highly traditional industry, I was immediately inspired by Janice's passion to focus on female clients, and by her commitment to educate and empower women. As a guest speaker at one of her events, I recognized early on that Janice understood the importance of creating a friendly environment to help women feel comfortable when talking and learning about money.

Janice's passion and vast financial experience is evident in *Let's Talk About Money: The Girlfriends' Guide to Protecting Her ASSets*. Her "girlfriend speak," combined with her personal stories and professional experience, bring important financial topics to life. Using her candid and authentic style, Janice helps women understand the WHY behind important financial issues and the HOW regarding the impact of these issues on their lives. Providing thought-provoking questions, Janice encourages women to engage in more meaningful conversations about money with friends, spouses, and family. By challenging antiquated notions about women and money, Janice eloquently guides women into a more pragmatic and healthy approach to managing their money and life. This groundbreaking book is a *must* read for every woman.

Adri Miller-Heckman
Women and Money Expert
Author of *The Keys to the Ladies' Room: A New Business Model for Financial Advisors*

Preface

Why I Had to Write This Book

Although I've been a financial expert for over thirty-two years and am a whiz at making my clients' money grow, I'll be the first to confess that I've made some pretty whopping financial mistakes in my personal life. I grew up in an environment where money was never discussed. And to be honest, I didn't really care, because my parents had plenty of it and I was their princess who never wanted for anything.

I'll come right out and say it: I was a spoiled brat. For those of you old enough to remember the movie *Private Benjamin*, I'm pretty sure the main character, the sheltered and well-to-do Judy Benjamin, was based on me.

After I received my bachelor's degree, I went straight to graduate school and earned a master's degree in counseling and guidance. Still unsure about what I wanted to do, I returned to graduate school and got a master's in non-profit business administration. I wasn't profit-motivated in the least, and earning an income wasn't at the top of my priorities because I'd just met and married a wonderful man. He was my Prince Charming, and he was going to take care of me for the rest of my life. I could return to my pampered Judy Benjamin life.

And then everything changed. Three short months after our wedding, my husband was diagnosed with leukemia. I naïvely assumed that my strong prince could win this battle, so I stayed optimistic. I was delusional about his chances of recovery and refused to allow the idea of his dying to enter my mind. However, leukemia prevailed and took my prince away from me forever.

Prior to my husband's diagnosis, we had been trying to get pregnant, and as fate would have it, I tested positive the day after I buried my beloved man. I was expecting not one child, but two.

I was a thirty-year-old widow, pregnant with twins.

When I had to file all of the paperwork after my husband's death, I was at a loss. I had no clue what I was supposed to do. I won't lie: I didn't even know how much money we had in our checking account or if we had multiple accounts. My husband was a very successful CPA, so there was no need for me to pay attention to any of these financial details—or so I had thought.

Then the other shoe dropped. After finally getting my husband's estate organized, I learned that he hadn't changed the beneficiary on his life insurance policy. The current beneficiary was his ex-wife. My twin boys and I were left with virtually nothing.

I had an important decision to make. I could either drown in grief and allow my boys to suffer the loss of their father, or I could get my ass in gear and start knocking on doors so my kids could live the life I'd always dreamed of them having. I wasted no time making that decision—I rolled up my sleeves like Rosie the Riveter and headed out to seek my family's fortunes and security.

Having lived this nightmare and knowing I needed to make a substantial income for my family, I chose to pursue work in the financial services industry. I also wanted to protect others from what I'd just experienced. I had been operating on the assumption that ignorance was bliss. What had happened to me made it decidedly clear this was *not* the case. So I made it my mission to educate women about finances.

Being a female in the financial industry during the early 1980s was a challenge. The industry wasn't just male-*dominated*—it was almost *entirely* male. Trying to break into the "old boys' club" wasn't easy. I frequently had doors slammed in my face and was often ridiculed for having the audacity to think I could have a career in finance.

I stood my ground and waited in offices from morning till night to show my eagerness. I wasn't going to take "no" for an answer. I didn't just *want* a job; I *needed* it for my boys. My maternal instinct to fight for my kids had kicked in full-blast, so I kept at it until I was finally offered an advisor position.

Once I got my foot in the door, I wasn't sure what to do next. I knew I had excellent ideas for building my business, but I felt intimated by all the testosterone surrounding me. I recall being the only woman at company lunches and board meetings. So many times I wanted to speak up and share my thoughts or offer an opinion, but I was afraid. I simply sat there in silence.

It wasn't until I found my voice that my wings began to grow— and then I *flew*. I discovered I had a gift for helping my female clients feel comfortable talking about money. Just like me before my husband died, many of them had never had to deal with financial matters, so I showed them that investing and retirement planning weren't rocket science and that you didn't need a doctorate in mathematics to understand your finances. My business soared, and before too long, my male colleagues began to see me as their equal.

Personally, I thought I was much higher than that!

Working with women in every situation imaginable has given me amazing insights into how we perceive, spend, invest, and save money. The common theme in the discussions I have with women is that they don't know *how* to talk about money.

Last year I conducted a seminar series called *Wonder Woman Wealth Creators*. After the first session, I asked my audience, a group of female professionals, if they had any questions.

Crickets. Total silence.

After a few minutes of the women looking around at each other, someone finally spoke up and said that she didn't know what questions to ask. The room suddenly filled with sounds of agreement. They all admitted that they wanted to ask questions, that they knew they were missing out on important information, but they didn't know *what* questions they should ask. This got me wondering if women don't like to talk about money because *they don't know what they don't know.* As a result, they keep their mouths shut and move on.

According to a 2013 Fidelity Investment study[1], women play a lesser role in financial decisions than men. They're considerably more likely to let their husbands meet with their financial advisors and handle all of the investment and retirement details. This is true not just for Boomers who grew up during the days of *Leave it to Beaver*. Gen X and Gen Y women assume an even smaller role in their family's day-to-day finances.

I want that to change!

After meeting with my *Wonder Woman Wealth Creators* crew, I realized that my new mission was to teach women how to ask the right financial questions. It's one thing to finally find the strength and chutzpah to speak up, but you also need to know how to speak the language, ask the right questions, and create a financial plan that works for *you.*

So I wrote this book because it's time women let their voices be heard. We've stayed silent far too long when it comes to finances, and if we're ever going to earn as much as our male counterparts, we have to start talking. When I look at my beautiful and talented daughter, who will someday encounter many of the challenges I've faced, I want to make sure she's armed with the financial knowledge to protect herself. I hope that *Let's Talk about Money: The Girlfriends' Guide to Protecting Her ASSets* provides you *and* her with both the chutzpah to speak up and the right questions to ask— so that you can protect your ASSets and create a bright financial future for yourself and your loved ones.

Janice Goldman
askjanicegoldman.com

---

[1] "2013 Couples Retirement Study Executive Summary." Fidelity Investments. 2013. Accessed May 14, 2016.
https://www.fidelity.com/static/dcle/welcome/documents/CouplesRetirementStudy.pdf

The moment a woman comes home to herself, the moment she knows that she has become a person of influence, an artist of her life, a sculptor of her universe, a person with rights and responsibilities who is respected and recognized, the resurrection of the world begins.

~ Joan D. Chittister

Chapter 1

Can We Talk?

The number one topic that women don't want to talk about is money. A recent Wells Fargo survey[2] found that 50 percent of women interviewed found it difficult to discuss their finances. It also revealed that women were less confident than men when it came to investing. To be fair it wasn't just women who were uncomfortable with money issues—for example, 38 percent of men were as well—and the title of the study drives home the point: "Conversations about personal finance more difficult than religion and politics." Similarly, another Fidelity Investments report[3] examining the "disconnect between couples" when discussing financial matters found that women tend to take a back seat in decision-making around household finances. Not only did they find that money is considered "the most challenging topic" to discuss, but eight out of ten women in the study said that they refrain from talking about money because they feel "uncomfortable" discussing it.

I understand this reasoning because I grew up in a time when talking about money was even more taboo than it is now. Although my parents never discussed our financial situation, as I mentioned

---

[2] "Conversations about Personal Finance More Difficult than Religion and Politics, According to New Wells Fargo Survey." February 20, 2014. Accessed May 11, 2016.
https://www.wellsfargo.com/about/press/2014/20140220_financial-health/
[3] "Tips for Women and Money - Fidelity Investments." March 23, 2016. Accessed May 11, 2016.
https://www.fidelity.com/viewpoints/personal-finance/women-manage-money

earlier I had no doubt that we had plenty of money.

I was born in 1951, when most women had four job options: teacher, nurse, secretary, or social worker. Although I wasn't encouraged to pursue a career beyond that of wife and mother, I always knew that I wanted something more than what was being offered.

My dad headed to his office every weekday morning like clockwork while my mom did her part by staying home to make sure dinner was served the minute he walked in the door. Mom also cleaned the house and ensured there was always a stock of homemade snacks ready when my two brothers and I returned from school. We were your typical '50s household—my mom baked the bread while dad earned it.

Even though my mom was treated like the village idiot because she didn't understand how to use the television remote, I knew that she was incredibly bright. I would sometimes overhear her talking to my dad about his business. I later discovered that she regularly advised him on it. If you had been living with us though, you'd have never known that my mother did anything besides make a killer brisket and keep the house immaculate.

I only caught snippets of my parents' hushed business discussions, but it was obvious that these conversations were for adults only. I didn't think much about this until I finally joined the rank of "adult" and was thrown into financial turmoil following the death of my first husband. It would have been incredibly helpful to have had financial insight from my parents as I struggled to make ends meet and embark on a career path that was dominated by men.

My mom taught me how to make a delicious broth for soup, but never once did she take me aside and explain the importance of setting up a household budget or the magic of compound interest. Funnily enough, she did tell me to have some "pushke" money, hidden funds kept in the house, usually for charity. But my mom wanted me to always have some of my own personal "pushke" money so I would have a feeling of freedom and independence.

And I wish my dad had taken me under his wing and coached

me on how to negotiate a starting salary or the importance of setting up a retirement account after getting a job. As a society though, we weren't taught how to have open discussions about money, so I don't blame my parents.

Let's Talk about the Gender Pay Gap

I first realized the importance of talking about money after my husband's death. I couldn't believe I'd been so naïve about my financial situation. And while that experience was a serious eye-opener for the need to have financial conversations, it was nothing compared to when I became the sole breadwinner for my family.

After eagerly accepting my first job in the financial industry, I soon learned that I was earning considerably less than the men in my office who were doing the same job I was doing. This became a defining moment for me. Although it took me quite a few years to speak up, I knew *then* that women had to begin talking about money.

The American Association of University Women (AAUW) recently reported that women are paid 21 percent less than men.[4] Let's think about this for a second. For every hour you work, girlfriends, you're only paid seventy-nine cents on the dollar. If you're paid $25 per hour, your male counterpart is paid $5.25 an hour more for doing the exact same job as you. Your taxable income is $1,000 per week, while your male colleague's is $1,210. Your annual earnings are $52,000, while your male coworker rakes in $12,920 more per year. And the gap is even greater if you're a woman of color. African American women earn 37 percent less, and Hispanic women or Latinas earn 46 percent less.

I don't know about you, but this really pisses me off.

Here's the thing that keeps me awake at night: *the pay gap isn't closing*. In fact, if it continues at its current rate, women won't receive equal pay for at least another *hundred years*. Not only will

---

[4] "The Simple Truth about the Gender Pay Gap (Spring 2016)." AAUW: Empowering Women Since 1881. 2016. Accessed June 05, 2016. http://www.aauw.org/research/the-simple-truth-about-the-gender-pay-gap/

the pay gap never close during my daughter's lifetime, but it probably still won't be closed during my grandchildren's lives.

This is just one reason why learning to have open discussions about finances is so important for women. Awareness and knowledge are power—whether we're talking about negotiating a better salary for ourselves, saving for retirement or putting our kids through college. We *need* to be well-informed and involved in order to create positive financial futures for ourselves and our children. How do we do this?

We start talking!

Women have stayed silent about money far too long—it's time to let our voices be heard.

Can I Really Ask That?

When I first broke down the doors of the "old boys' club" thirty-two years ago, I never uttered a word at meetings and company lunches. There were so many times when I wanted to chime in on a conversation, but I was too intimidated to add my two cents. And then one day it hit me—if I didn't start to speak up, I might lose the opportunity. I knew that I had important things to say, and by golly, I wasn't going to miss my chance. No one says it better than New York Senator Kirsten Gillibrand in her book *Off the Sidelines: Raise Your Voice, Change the World.* She writes, "If you don't speak up, then a woman's perspective may never get heard."

There's a double-standard when it comes to men and women speaking their minds. Men are viewed as wise and strong. Women are often seen as just being "bitches." But in order to start taking charge of our own financial futures—not to mention our lives—we have to stop *not* asking questions or speaking out because we're afraid people won't like us. It's time to start protecting ourselves. And if that makes us less "likeable" to some people, they're probably not who we want to hang out with anyway.

The first thing I want you to do is to *start asking questions*. If you don't understand something about your finances or if you sense something isn't as it should be—ASK! You should never ever *ever* agree to anything if you're unsure what's being asked of you. Asking questions doesn't make you "stupid" or "bitchy." Quite the contrary! Knowledge is power, and the best way to acquire this control is by asking questions.

If we want to make greater strides at closing the gender wage and wealth gaps, we have to start speaking out and end the money talk taboo. There is absolutely nothing wrong with:

- Asking why the man doing the exact same job as you is earning 21 percent *more* than you.
- Asking your future partner what debts he has and about his FICO score.
- Talking to your parents about their estate.
- Telling your adult children they have to pay rent if they return home.

In fact, there is everything *right* about speaking your mind on these and similar matters. Every single one of them has a potentially huge impact on your financial future, and probably that of your family as well. You owe it to yourself to *ask*.

So, yes, you can . . . and *should* have these conversations! Protect your financial well-being. Discussions about money keep your bank account healthy!

"Why Do I Make Less Than My Male Co-Stars?"

One of my favorite outspoken women of the decade is actress Jennifer Lawrence. Following the infamous Sony Pictures hack in 2015—one result of which was the release of salary information for some of Hollywood's top stars—the actress caused an uproar by publishing "Why Do I Make Less Than My Male Co-Stars?"[5] This scathing essay tackled the pay disparity between male and female cast members of the movie *American Hustle*.

---

[5] Lawrence, Jennifer. "Why Do I Make Less Than My Male Co-Stars?" Lenny Letter. October 14, 2015. Accessed May 11, 2016. http://www.lennyletter.com/work/a147/jennifer-lawrence-why-do-i-make-less-than-my-male-costars/

In her essay, Lawrence notes that she "didn't want to seem 'difficult' or 'spoiled' when negotiating her contract." Well, that was until she discovered that her male co-stars "definitely didn't worry about being 'difficult' or 'spoiled.'" She continues by assuming her male colleagues "were commended for being fierce and tactical, while I was busy worrying about coming across as a brat and not getting my fair share." Commenting on a leaked Sony email referring to a lead actress as a "spoiled brat," Jennifer writes, "For some reason, I just can't picture someone saying that about a man."

Lawrence blamed herself for her lack of negotiation skills and her desire to be likable. Well, no more *Little Miss Nice*. Lawrence writes, "I'm over trying to find the 'adorable' way to state my opinion and still be likable! Fuck that. I don't think I've ever worked for a man in charge who spent time contemplating what angle he should use to have his voice heard. It's just heard."

Bring it, women. We have to speak up for what we want and need. Let our voices rise!

Step Out of Your Comfort Zone

I firmly believe that most women haven't learned that the rich are rich because they have their money working *for* them. You can't simply let your money sit there and do nothing. No, if you want to increase your money, you have to put it to work.

Through my years in the financial industry, I've discovered that women aren't risk-takers. The problem with this is that when there's no risk, there's no potential for reward or growth. I'm not saying you should pull your savings and start blindly playing the stock market. However, if women are going to get a leg-up financially, they have to start taking some chances with their money.

Back in 2004, a number of my female clients became involved in investment clubs. They wanted to handle that aspect of their family's finances. The clubs were going great until the financial crisis of 2007-08. This is when all of the markets went off track with the collapse of the housing and mortgage markets. Many economists consider it the worst financial crisis since the Great Depression.

Prior to this, these women had really been getting the hang of investing. They loved researching the different stocks, comparing growth—and making money.

Then: BAM!

The financial crisis hit, and the investment clubs immediately shut down.

Suddenly the women no longer wanted to be responsible for their family's investments. They were scared off by the financial crisis. I'll never forget the time I called a client and she told me that she wanted her husband to make all the investment decisions from now on because she was too nervous about the market.

It's not my intention here to downplay the severity of the global financial crisis at the time, but it was certainly true that with stocks at rock-bottom prices it was the perfect climate for investing. It was like Black Friday on the market. Citigroup stock, which is currently selling for approximately $40, was listed at *$3 per share*. Investors who got out there and *bought* instead of sold made massive amounts of money. A $3,000 investment could turn into a $37,000 profit.

As Warren Buffet says, "Buy when there's blood in the streets." It's no time to put your head in the sand or hide behind your husband's pant leg.

Get out there and learn, girlfriends! You don't want to follow the herd. Don't be afraid to take chances with some of your cash. Join an investment club, financial book group, or enroll in an Investing 101 class at a local community college.

Let's Get this Party Started!

Are you ready to start talking? Prepare to get down and dirty as we talk about marriage and divorce, parents and children, making money and paying taxes, and so much more. I've invited a group of outstanding experts to chime in with their own advice and opinions. I've also created checklists and a wrap-up of each chapter. The whole point is to learn while having fun along the way, so I hope you'll keep this book by your financial bedside or in your purse so you can refer to it whenever you need insight and support for the crucial money discussions in your life.

We don't know what we don't know—and what we don't know will hurt us. This book provides the questions you don't know so you can find the answers you need to stay protected and build a bright financial future for yourself.

Let's start talking!

The

 5

Most Important

Discussions

to Have about Money

Let's Talk about Relationships

[Women] associate financial rescue, or living happily ever after, with satisfaction of emotional needs. They are afraid that abandoning the rescue fantasy also means abandoning the possibility of love.

Annette Lieberman
Unbalanced Accounts

Chapter 2

Let's Get Naked . . . Financially:
Talking about Money with Your Partner
Before and After Marriage

It's amazing how much easier it is to get *physically* naked with your partner than it is to get *financially* naked. Many couples sometimes first approach the money conversation when they consider living together, but surprisingly, the topic is often skated over even then. While I think it's critical you and your partner talk about money when you make such a drastic relationship transition, I also feel it's an incredibly important conversation to have much earlier than this.

Maybe you're constantly getting stuck with the check for drinks, or maybe your new beau prefers to go Dutch on dinner or pay your way every time. Whatever the case, it's never too soon to talk about who's paying for what. And don't get me wrong—I'm not saying that one person should always foot the bill, nor am I suggesting you conduct a formal financial interview before your first date—leave some room for spontaneity here! But in general, it *does* help to be aware of these things and to know ahead of time what your fiscal responsibility will be for a date. I know many women—heck, I've been one of them—who spent a fortune preparing for a date only to unexpectedly wind up paying for dinner. If you establish an agreement before the event, then you know what to expect.

Ground Rules for Getting Naked

Whether you've hooked up on an online dating site or met at a friend's party, if you've become a "couple," it's time to talk about money. Couples are people who repeatedly date, and who at some point have probably gotten physically naked together. They've most likely discussed sex, politics, family, religion and whether or not they want kids. So why on earth do so many people leave talking about personal finances until much later, if ever?

Well, that's got to change. It's time to bare your financial souls and get *fiscally* naked.

Before you initiate the discussion, ground rules need to be established. First, there must be trust. In order for you and your partner to feel comfortable sharing the good, bad, and possibly ugly aspects of your financial lives, it's important that you feel safe during the disclosure. This means no laughter, snide remarks, or judgments regarding prior financial decisions. It's potentially a little scary to share this side of yourself, and the last thing anyone needs is to be made fun of for bad investments or overspending. The idea here is to feel safe enough that should either of you have financial ghosts in your closet you feel relaxed enough to bring them into the light of day.

The next rule is total honesty. You both need to be completely forthright as you strip down and get financially naked. If you've had to file for bankruptcy or have a history of compulsive shopping, now is the time to divulge this information to your partner. If you've got a mountain of debt or a financial obligation from a previous relationship, your partner needs to know. And you should feel comfortable requesting this information from them as well. There are to be no secrets or "tiny, little lies" during this conversation. Otherwise, what's the point?

Opening the door to the money talk isn't as painful as you might think. After you establish the ground rules—trust and honesty— you're ready to get naked. And just as physical sex can bring two people closer together, discussing your financial history can open the door to a new level of intimacy. It's not all about dollar signs.

Our relationship with money reflects different aspects of ourselves, and this is one of the reasons why sharing information about our finances can make us feel vulnerable.

There are several ways to open the discussion. For example, were any lessons learned about money during previous relationships? Did a former partner need to work too much to make ends meet—and was therefore less available emotionally? Or did debt contribute to the breakup of the relationship? You could also start the chat by discussing financial goals and values. Or maybe you have a bit of a . . . *quirky* financial past yourself. If so, it's time to inform your partner about your money mishaps.

Another way to start the conversation is to ask for financial advice. Start out by saying that you've been trying to learn more about making financial decisions and would like to know your partner's thoughts about saving versus investing. After the ice has been broken, get a little more personal and ask your partner what he or she thinks about your spending habits and if there are any changes he or she might suggest. A few days later, you might open the discussion to debt—should you pay off your consumer debt or student loan debt first? The goal is to open the pipeline to future conversations about money and to show your partner that financial discussions are important to you.

There is a two-fold purpose to these dialogues. One, you need to enter the relationship with your eyes wide open so that you know what you're getting yourself into financially. When you become a partnership, your partner's expenses become *your* expenses, whether you want them to or not. Two, you *want* to work together financially. According to a TD Bank study on love and money,[6] couples who talk about money regularly are considerably happier than those who don't. Forty-two percent of those who discuss finances on a weekly basis described their relationship as "extremely happy," compared to 27 percent of those who have these

---

[6] "TD Bank Surveys and Research." TD Bank News, Press Releases, Media Relations, Media Room. June 2015. Accessed May 11, 2016.
https://mediaroom.tdbank.com/couplesoverview

conversations less than once a month.

It's important to begin talking about finances early on in order to give due consideration to the role they'll be playing in the relationship. If your partner is committed to ten years' worth of child support from a previous relationship, you need to know this.

Now, I don't want to imply that these kinds of financial discussions will always reveal skeletons in the closet. Everything may be hunky-dory with both of your finances. If that's the case—great! It will be a relief to find yourselves on the same financial page so you can begin looking forward to a financially secure future together. Nor do I want to say that if either of you *do* have skeletons in your closets it's time to split. Far from it. It's just important to be *aware* early on to avoid unpleasant surprises.

I have a client, "Tessa," who is a notorious Amazon addict. No kidding. I suspect Tessa has an Amazon drone permanently assigned to deliver parcels to her address. When her relationship with "Josh" became serious, Tessa fessed up to her obsession. Fortunately, she had an income to support her habit, but it was important for Josh to know about this before they moved in together.

Talking about money with your partner can sometimes be a deal maker or a deal *breaker*. A friend of mine, "Jessica," met a really nice man, "Tom," on an online dating site. They had been dating for over a month when Jessica took my advice and told Tom that she wanted to talk about money. Both were in their late forties and had been married before. At first, Tom was hesitant to talk about his financial past. To get the conversation started, Jessica told Tom that she had finally paid off her considerable credit card debt the previous year. Tom was impressed and told her that he doesn't use credit cards because he and his ex-wife had filed for bankruptcy during their marriage, and now he's wary of credit.

Tom's confession about being in bankruptcy could have sent Jessica running for the door—especially if she had learned of it when they were trying to lease an apartment or buy a home together. However, a new level of trust developed in their relationship because Tom opened up about his financial situation. And Tom, of course, was reassured to find that Jessica was debt-free and had learned a lesson about staying that way.

I won't lie: some financial issues can be real deal breakers. So whether you or your partner have bad credit scores, past bankruptcies, exorbitant credit card or student loan debts, alimony or child support payments, it's better to find out before you become too serious.

Financial ignorance is *not* bliss!

Are You Financially Compatible?

It can definitely be a little intimidating to crack open that Pandora's Box of past financial blunders, but doing so makes for a much healthier and stronger relationship. In addition to learning more about your partner's financial past, talking about money allows you to determine whether or not you're financially compatible. The number one cause of divorce is money, and much of the time this is because couples don't share the same financial goals. I assure you, you'll encounter a great deal of stress if you're a saver and your partner is a spendthrift. I'm not saying it won't work, but it's best to know this before you sublet your apartment, walk down the aisle or, heaven forbid, receive your first joint credit card bill.

I once worked with a couple, "Andrea" and "Martin," who had totally opposite views of money and how to spend it. Money was very tight when Andrea was growing up. Her father was often hired on contract, and there would be months of unemployment between jobs, so Andrea's family relied on government assistance and sometimes a local food bank throughout her childhood. She not only saw what poverty was like—she lived it. Martin, on the other hand, never had a hungry day in his life. He grew up in an affluent neighborhood and vacationed every summer at his family's Cape Cod beach house. His parents gave him a new BMW when he graduated from law school.

When Andrea and Martin came to see me, Andrea expressed concern that they should be saving and investing more money. She was also annoyed that Martin refused to maintain a household budget. She complained that Martin would "just go out and buy whatever he wanted, whenever he wanted" without consulting her. In addition, Martin insisted they set up a trust fund for their future children. Andrea confessed that she wasn't keen on the idea because "only rich kids" have trust funds, and she didn't want her children to feel entitled.

Andrea and Martin had never talked about their financial aspirations prior to getting married, so I asked them individually about their financial goals. Andrea's only desire was to save money. Martin was on-board with saving, but he also wanted to enjoy their substantial income by living in a beautiful home and traveling around the world. Andrea saw such activities as luxuries and was content to live in a modest house and limit their travel to locations in the United States in order to increase their savings.

At first glance, this couple might have seemed as though they were financially incompatible. However, I thought they were actually quite a good match. I could see Andrea's point about saving money, especially with a husband who wanted to change BMWs every two years. I could also see that, in Andrea's case, growing up in such a precarious financial environment was enough to make anyone frugal.

On the other hand, I understood Martin's frustration with Andrea's insistence that they devote such a large portion of their income to investments and savings. Martin felt he'd earned his right to new cars and vacations abroad.

What I saw was that Andrea's frugality kept Martin grounded while Martin's desire to have fun made Andrea's life much more meaningful.

I asked Andrea how much money it would take for her to feel secure. After calculating their monthly expenses, Andrea announced that she needed $500,000 in the bank before she would relax. Looking at the couple's portfolio, I informed her that they were actually quite close to this amount. Andrea gasped as I shared the news. Although she regularly reviewed their quarterly reports, she had never thought about their savings balance and the amount of money it would take for her to relinquish her fear of having the kinds of money problems she had encountered in her youth. I assured Andrea that she and Martin were in very good financial shape and that they should begin enjoying their life together.

Financial compatibility doesn't mean that you and your partner have the same spending and savings habits. In fact, that's often a formula for disaster; imagine what could happen to a spendthrift married to a spendthrift. What you actually want is to share similar financial goals—and strategies for achieving them. Just as opposites tend to attract, it's usually a good thing when a spender marries a saver. If they work together and compromise, they can do both—spend and save—in moderation. It's like having your cake and eating it, too.

Love and Money are Two Different Things

Many women I've spoken to tell me that marriage is what they dream about because they "want to be rescued." A dear friend once confided that she wanted to find a husband so she could be financially secure. Well, I'm here to tell you, love and financial security don't go hand-in-hand.

We talked above about having that fiscally naked conversation, about sharing your past activities, your present habits, and your future plans. Even after that general conversation, before you and your partner approach the idea of cohabitation, there are many specific financial details you'll want to get straight on. For example, the first question will be how you'll split the household expenses and rent or mortgage. Having this discussion isn't romantic in the least, but always remember: love and money are two different things. On the other hand, they *are* usually connected. And I promise that if you talk about money *now*, there will be room for a whole lot more love later.

In addition to dividing the expenses, you'll want to create an overview of your debts and assets. If your partner is entering into the relationship with significant student loan debt or maxed-out credit cards, you need to know this. It's a great idea to find out your partner's credit score.

C'mon, think of it this way: before you slept together, you hopefully ensured your partner was STD-free. Well, think of credit scores the same way. You want to make sure there are no hidden diseases in your partner's financial past. When you get financially naked, it's important to examine your partner's **S**alary, **T**axes, and **D**ebt!

Credit Scores

If you and your partner are ever planning to buy a home or make a major purchase together, it's imperative you know your credit scores. You don't want to fall madly in love with someone only to discover that they have bad credit. This could impact your future together dramatically. I've worked with women who have made this very mistake, and I assure you, it's much easier to be *proactive* about the situation than *reactive*. Protect yourself and make sure your partner has decent credit.

Your credit score is primarily based on three things:

- The money you've borrowed.
- The amount you owe.
- Whether or not you're making payments on time.

The thing about your credit score is this: it can make or break your future happiness. No kidding. This three-digit number is the key that opens doors to everything from having the ability to obtain a loan, rent an apartment, connect utilities, purchase insurance, and even get a job. This isn't a joke, and if you don't know your partner's credit score before you get seriously involved, you're potentially setting yourself up for some difficult times in the future.

Fortunately, obtaining a credit report is easier now than it ever has been. Many credit card companies provide this as a free service to their customers. Also, the website www.annualcreditreport.com offers exactly what their name suggests: a free annual credit report. There are quite a few different credit reporting companies, but the most common is FICO. If someone asks about your credit score, they're usually referring to this score. FICO scores are based on information obtained from the three major reporting agencies: Equifax, Experian, and TransUnion. They range from 300 to 850. A score of 781 and above is considered excellent, while 600 or below is considered poor. Having excellent credit not only assures you of the ability to obtain loans, but it also makes it more likely you'll be offered the best interest rates.

In other words, it *pays* to have good credit.

Karen's Story

It's very easy to fall prey to bad judgment when you're in the throes of blossoming love. The thing about money and love is that they're both emotionally charged topics, and if you're not careful, you can make some really horrible decisions. A friend, "Karen," had been dating "Bruce" for nearly a year. Both had recently divorced, so they were eager to get on with their lives. Although there wasn't a wedding date set, the couple had started to look for houses. Bruce was renting an apartment, and Karen planned to sell the large home that she'd gotten in the divorce. They were looking for a smaller, more modest house close to Karen's mother. Karen was so excited to start life over again with Bruce.

Several months later, Karen called to tell me that she and Bruce had broken up. It turns out he had been unemployed throughout the majority of their relationship, and during this time, he had borrowed nearly $20,000 from her. Although she said this wasn't the cause of the break-up, I suspect it definitely played a role. I asked if Bruce had paid her back with interest. Karen sheepishly confessed that he hadn't paid *any* of his loan back.

Before you make comments or judge her, I want you to know that Karen is a very bright doctor with a thriving medical practice— she's a smart woman with good business sense. But she had fallen in love, and that thrill clouded her judgment on money issues. As Karen explained through tears, she was looking for houses with him—she thought he was "the one." It had never occurred to her that she'd been taken for a ride by her handsome beau. At least she'd discovered the truth *before* they'd walked down the aisle.

So *please* remember: love and money are two different things.

Love shouldn't have anything to do with money, and vice versa. This is why it's never okay for you to lend money to someone you're dating. I don't care if they say you're the most beautiful woman in the world—don't lend them money! The same can be said for co-signing for your partner, getting a loan in your name, or making a large joint purchase together.

Don't do it!

If money changes hands, it needs to be done with signed legal documents. Even then it's important to know that money can destroy relationships, whether between lovers or friends.

Use caution when sharing your wealth.

Before You Say "Yes" to the Dress

So let's say things between you and your partner have zipped along to the point where you're engaged. You're completely elated, planning for the wedding and whatever comes next.

And then your partner utters the frightening "P" word.

You're totally taken off guard. Questions race through your mind: you're not marrying a movie star or a billionaire, so why should you need to sign a *prenuptial agreement?* Aren't you trustworthy? How incredibly unromantic!

Wait a second!

Before you act offended and adopt a defensive attitude, consider what a prenup does to protect not just your future partner's assets, but your own as well.

Marriage is far more than simply two people vowing to love each other until death they do part. Marriage is a partnership where each party needs to know what the other brings to the relationship. So in this sense, a prenup is a *foundation-builder*.

And let's be honest: you need to start your marriage on solid ground.

A prenup provides newlyweds with a solid financial foundation because it offers a clear picture of what they have so that they can jointly plan for a wonderful future together. I think a prenuptial agreement is a wonderful idea, though I also feel it should be called a *clarity document* because that's what it does: provides clarity on a couple's financial life. What's unromantic about planning for a bright future together?

Talking about the Prenup

Whether it's you or your future partner who utters the "P" word, it's a discussion that needs to take place before you walk down the aisle. The best time to broach the subject of a prenup is when you're getting naked financially with your partner. Having created a safe environment for the financial discussion, you have the perfect opportunity to mention that you will want your future partner to sign a prenup. If this announcement surprises your partner, reassure them that it's simply a form of insurance and nothing personal. Marriage is a business transaction, and like anything in business, you want to ensure your assets are protected.

You can also approach the discussion as I mentioned above by sharing the idea that a prenup can serve as a foundational document for a marriage. Once the financial details are out in the open and mutually understood, you can both look forward with clarity. After all, money has been shown to be a major source of breakups, so getting on the same page at the beginning can be seen as putting your best foot forward for a long and successful future together.

Lauren's Story

A successful client of mine named "Lauren" was preparing to marry "Troy." When I asked Lauren if she had a prenup, she looked stunned and gave me the whole "it's unromantic" spiel. I explained that romance has nothing to do with a prenup and that money discussions are a form of intimacy couples should have on a regular basis. I asked her if she knew much about her future husband's assets and debts.

Again, Lauren was slightly taken aback because her future husband had a successful career and appeared to be financially sound. She sheepishly asked if I was implying Troy might be hiding something from her. I assured her that I wasn't suggesting deceit, but I reminded her that throughout my many years in the financial industry, I'd met quite a few clients who had entered into a marriage without a clear picture of their future spouses' finances. Many were surprised to find out down the road that their new spouses weren't as financially sound as they had once appeared.

Lauren, still reluctant, assured me that Troy had a nice house in a very affluent neighborhood. I asked if she knew how much the mortgage was and what the interest rate was on the house. Would she be paying part of the mortgage, and if so, would the deed would be in her name as well as his?

Flustered by my questions, Lauren admitted she hadn't thought of this. She had instead been focused on wedding preparations like dress fittings and floral arrangements. I assured her that she could continue with her wedding plans, but she also needed to find time to have a financial talk with her future husband.

Taking my advice, Lauren opened the financial conversation with her future spouse. She informed Troy that her financial advisor had suggested they write a prenuptial agreement so that they could begin their married life with a clear financial picture and a solid financial foundation.

Did her beloved run out of the room or call off the wedding?

No.

In fact, they are happily married with a prenuptial agreement that ensures that each of them understands their individual and joint financial situations.

After all, what man doesn't want a strong woman who knows how to look out for herself and her assets?

It's Time to Rethink the Prenup

Let's face it: you've worked hard for your money and good

credit score. Unless you know what your future spouse is bringing into the marriage, you risk losing both. I understand that the idea of marriage is still steeped in some longstanding, antiquated beliefs. Hey, it wasn't that long ago when a woman was considered the property of her husband! As such, she had very few (if any) legal rights.

Well, it's the twenty-first century, girlfriends, and you *most definitely* have rights—so use them!

You might ask what you should do if your future spouse refuses to talk about money or if the mention of a prenuptial agreement causes an argument. Well, of course it's up to you whether or not to press on with the discussion, but I'd like to remind you that marriage is more than a bond of love between two people—marriage is also a legal agreement. Once you and your beloved are betrothed, you legally become a partnership. I would hope it would be an *equal* partnership. Think about it this way: would you start a company with someone without knowing what he or she was bringing into the business?

Of course you wouldn't!

So why in the world would you start a marriage without such vital information?

Still Not Convinced You Need a Prenup?

Do we need to keep talking? Okay, let me ask you this: what is the number one cause of divorce in the United States?

Infidelity?

Marrying too young?

Nope. The number one cause of divorce is *money*. Nearly 50 percent of divorce is due to financial issues.[7] Furthermore, nearly 65 percent of couples argue about money on a regular basis.

The ball is in your court. I urge you not to be a statistic in the

---

[7] "U.S. Divorce Rates and Statistics - Divorce Stats." Accessed May 11, 2016. http://www.divorcesource.com/ds/main/u-s-divorce-rates-and-statistics-1037.shtml

battle over money.

Personally, I think prenuptial agreements have gotten a bum rap, especially thanks to the media. Stop thinking that a prenup is your future partner's code for "I think she's a gold digger" or "I don't trust him." Instead, think of a prenup as a type of insurance policy that protects your separate property, future inheritances, maintenance (or alimony), insurance, future income, trust interests, retirement funds, and so much more. See what I mean? A prenup is little more than an insurance policy for the couple and their existing and potential children. The bottom line is that a prenuptial agreement protects your premarital assets and the income and assets you acquire as a couple, and in the event of divorce, it determines who gets what. Have I persuaded you to rethink the prenup? Let me throw a few more statistics your way. According to a 2013 survey of the American Academy of Matrimonial Lawyers[8], divorce attorneys have seen a 63 percent increase in prenuptial agreements over the past three years. And get this: the survey reported that there was a 46 percent increase in *women* asking for prenups. I predict this trend will continue to rise as women become more successful and the stigma of a prenuptial agreement decreases.

Finally, let me reiterate that a prenup doesn't just protect your material assets. No, a prenup provides insurance for your future children and *their* assets. Not only does it ensure your children's assets are protected, but also their emotions: with a prenup, there is less chance of a nasty divorce settlement.

While you should never enter into a union with the anticipation that it will end, there is absolutely nothing wrong with making plans for that very possibility. It's not "unromantic" or "distrustful" to ask for a prenuptial agreement; it's just plain common sense. You don't buy home insurance because you think your house is going to catch on fire. You buy it for protection *just in case* it does.

This is exactly what a prenuptial agreement is: protection. A

---

[8] "Older Brides, Grooms, Lead to Increase in Prenuptial Agreements." AAML National. July 6, 2010. Accessed June 08, 2016.
http://www.aaml.org/about-the-academy/press/aaml-in-the-news/pre-post-nuptial-agreements/older-brides-grooms-lead-increa.

prenuptial agreement doesn't cause couples to split. Growing apart emotionally, infidelity, financial problems, and incompatibility— these are the real reasons why most couples divorce, not the prenup. The prenup is there just in case the unexpected happens and you *do* break-up.

Making Money Conversations a Habit

Starting your relationship on a firm financial footing is one of the best ways to ensure a lasting union. And the sooner you start talking openly about finances, rather than treating them as a dirty secret that should only be avoided or argued about, the easier it is to *keep* talking. Make it a habit to regularly check in with each other on household finances. Bumps in the road are inevitable, but if you have already established that it's better to talk about them than ignore them and hope they'll go away, you'll forge an even stronger bond.

Questions for Getting Naked Financially and Talking About the Prenup

Compatibility

1. What are your financial goals and values?

2. Describe your money style. Are you a compulsive buyer?

3. Do you maintain a budget?

Prenup

4. What assets are being brought into the relationship?

5. What debts are being brought into the relationship? Be sure to include student loan, business loan, credit card, and any other debts that could impact the relationship.

6. What is your credit score?

7. How will you handle the funds as a couple? What accounts will be joint and what will be his and hers?

8. How will the expenses be divided?

9. How will the housing expenses be divided?

10. What are your financial obligations to your and your partner's children? Does your partner pay child support? If your partner has children from a previous marriage, is he or she committed by divorce decree to pay for his or her child's private school or college?

11. Does your partner pay alimony or have other obligations from another relationship? If either of you were married before, you want to read over the divorce decree to make sure you understand the financial obligations of the decree and any impact they could have on the present relationship.

12. Do either of you have a planned inheritance or trust? Will these funds be shared? If so, how? If an inheritance always stays in one partner's name, it's not considered a "joint asset."

13. Who are the beneficiaries and owners of all the life insurance policies and annuities, pensions, retirement accounts, and other policies? Only the owner of the policy can make changes to the beneficiary.

14. Is the amount of insurance sufficient? If either of you are bringing children into the marriage, you will want to review both health and life policies.

15. Do you need to update or change your wills?

16. Do you need to update or change the titling of property?

17. Think hard about other financial issues that should be discussed in advance. Do you or your partner have expensive hobbies? Plans to go back to school? A job where the income varies month-to-month? Try to anticipate challenges in advance so you can make a plan to tackle them together.

Let's Hear from the Experts

Katie C. Galanes

Katie C. Galanes is a Family Law Attorney with Grunyk & Associates, a Naperville, Illinois law firm.

What's the number one mistake couples make when they cohabitate?

The number one mistake couples make when cohabitating is assuming the other person's financial information. Typically, couples avoid discussing money or finances because these are taboo subjects. However, it is imperative that the couple gets on the same page when it comes to each other's financial information and their realistic ability to contribute to household expenses. A common mistake couples make when cohabitating is treating their financial identity separately. Once you begin residing with one another and become serious in your relationship, it is incredibly important to start seeing yourselves as a team. In order to be the best functioning team, you need to share information and treat your financial identity as *one unit*. If you are going to borrow money or get a loan together, buy a house together, get a joint bank account together, or associate yourself in any way with the other person financially, you should discuss financial issues with one another before that process occurs.

What are some non-threatening ways to discuss your financials with your significant other?

One strategy is to ask about future planning. You can bring up a topic that is something you may aspire to in the future, such as purchasing a home or having children, and ask if the financial support will be there at that future date or if you will both need to plan ahead financially for these things. Another strategy is to discuss the lifestyle and hobbies of your significant other. You can think about what they like to do in their spare time and, if your partner's hobbies are expensive or he or she vacations frequently, you can discuss how continuing to do so after you're a committed couple will affect your joint finances.

How will I know if the person I am with is a good financial match?

One way to gauge this is to examine hobbies, spending habits, comments when incurring an expense, personality, values and more. These considerations will help you determine whether the person is a saver or an excessive spender. A good way to avoid problems with regards to finances is to openly discuss financial information. Frequently, when one person is a saver and very conservative with their money while the other person spends extensively and lacks any kind of budget, it leads to divorce because neither person is on the same page about managing finances as the other. Communication is key here, as is coming up with a financial strategy that works best for both parties involved. For example, if you are an excessive spender and the other person is a saver, it may be a good idea to create a household budget of monthly income and expenses and come up with a monthly allotment for spending purposes separate from joint expenses. Also, decide on some mutually agreed goals that you both want. These can include retirement accounts, emergency savings, down payment for a home, vacation home, and so on. These are all good automatic funds to set up so that there isn't that much extra money left over to squabble about.

What are red flags in a relationship that can lead to problems in the future when it comes to getting financially naked with one another?

When someone will not openly discuss their financial information, whether that means discussing their income, expenses, assets or liabilities, it is a red flag. If you are trying to have an open discussion with your significant other and they refuse to discuss the topic or answer questions, this could mean that they are embarrassed or hiding something from their financial past.

Janice L. Boback

Janice L. Boback is a managing partner of the law firm of Anderson & Boback, a Chicago law firm which specializes in domestic relations.

How does a prenuptial agreement work and what does it cover?

A prenuptial agreement is a contract entered into between two people who are engaged to be married. The contract can cover anything that the parties want it to cover except for child support and custody of their future children. Each couple has their own specific set of circumstances and those circumstances determine what should be covered in a prenuptial agreement.

What should we include in the prenuptial agreement?

A prenuptial agreement should include anything you want to remove from litigation in the event of a divorce. For example, if the bride-to-be has inherited a house which is in her name only, it should be listed in the prenuptial agreement stating that it shall remain her non-marital property. In the event of a divorce, the prenuptial agreement will keep the husband from arguing that the property became marital because they lived in it, fixed it up, he did work on the property, etc. A prenuptial agreement simply takes an issue off the table during a dissolution of marriage. This means preservation of more marital money with less attorney fees.

Do we need to see an attorney to write a prenuptial agreement or can we DIY it?

Both parties to a prenuptial agreement must be represented by their own attorney. This will protect the document's integrity in the event it is challenged during a divorce. If one of the parties was not represented at the time the prenuptial agreement was created, the court could construe the document as being unenforceable.

We're already married without a prenuptial agreement. Is it too late to get one now?

Because both pre- and postnuptial agreements are contracts, all contracts require what is called "consideration"—something of value that each person provides. Without consideration, a contract is invalid. It is too late to get a prenuptial agreement after the marriage. The consideration for a prenuptial is *the marriage*. Consideration is an essential element for a contract. After a marriage, the parties can still be entered into a contract similar to a prenuptial agreement, but since it is *after* the marriage, it is called a postnuptial agreement. Again, there must be consideration. Consideration is something of value given by both parties that induces them to enter into the contract. Consideration may consist of a promise to do something or a promise to refrain from doing something that you are legally entitled to do. An example of a postnuptial consideration might be spousal or child support.

Wrap-Up

*Why You Need to Get Financially Naked with
Your Partner and Rethink the Prenup*

1. It's never too early to get *fiscally* naked with your partner. Just as you'd never sleep with someone before knowing if they have STDs, the same is true in regards to money. You need to know that your future partner is credit-worthy and financially stable.

2. Set ground rules before you get financially naked. It's important to create an environment of trust and be completely honest with your partner. There should be no judgement or "little white lies" when talking about money.

3. Money is the number one cause of divorce, but it's also the least-discussed topic. A strong relationship is built on financial compatibility. Ensure that you and your partner have similar financial goals and values.

4. Love and money are two different animals. Don't confuse love with money or money with love. They need to be separate in order to have a strong relationship. It's easy to be so overcome by love that you make bad decisions when finances enter the picture.

5. Don't ever lend money, co-sign, or obtain a loan for your future partner. These actions lead to only one thing—trouble!

6. A prenuptial agreement provides a solid financial foundation for newlyweds. As a result, the couple can begin their married life with a plan for their future.

7. A prenuptial agreement acts as an insurance policy for you and your fiancé. The prenup protects your premarital assets, income, and assets you acquire as a married couple and indicates who gets what in the event of death or divorce.

8. A prenuptial agreement offers a clear financial picture of both parties prior to marriage. There are no financial surprises after you say "I do." So in this sense, a prenuptial

agreement removes any financial secrets from the relationship. It's a real opportunity to "get naked" with your future partner.

9. A prenuptial agreement protects and clarifies the children's and grandchildren's inheritance rights from a former marriage.

Chapter 3

Divorce and Remarriage with Eyes Wide Open: No More Little Miss Nice, Little Miss Naïve, and Little Miss Delusional

Okay, I've been there, done that, so I know all too well that divorce isn't easy. Of course it depends on your situation, but making the decision to end a marriage is often very difficult and sometimes quite scary. Whether the choice was yours or your partner's, it's critical that you're ready for what lies ahead before, during, and after the divorce.

Nobody wants to prepare for a divorce, but let me tell you, much like any major life event, you need to do some groundwork before you initiate the process. I don't know if you've gone for counseling, but this, of course, is my first recommendation. One thing to keep in mind as you consider divorce is that most states and the Social Security Administration consider ten years of marriage a "long-term" marriage. As a result, depending on your circumstances, you might be eligible for additional Social Security benefits as well as increased alimony. However, if you know for certain that you and your partner are going to split, the first thing I urge you to do is get your financial affairs in order.

Can You Afford to Get Divorced?

Money is the number one cause of stress in a marriage, and I assure you, if you're struggling financially as a couple, it's not going to get any easier when you begin divorce proceedings.[9] In fact, many couples who end a marriage due to money problems often find themselves in bankruptcy court. Divorce is one of the most common reasons listed for filing bankruptcy.[10] According to the Association of Public Policy and Management, there is a direct correlation between divorce and bankruptcy. It's no wonder that many couples joke they can't afford to get divorced. Sadly, this is often true. I know a couple who got married four years ago and who can barely stand the sight of each other now. No kidding—"Janette" and "John" fight like cats and dogs. Unfortunately, they jointly own a home, and due to an upside-down mortgage and high housing costs, they can't afford to sell or move out. John lives on one side of the house while Janette occupies the other. It's an awkward situation, but it's also a very common one.

I've also had women tell me that they didn't hire an attorney, not only because they couldn't afford one, but also because there were minimal assets involved. I have a client, "Cynthia," who had been married to "Joe" for twenty-four years. During this time, Joe emotionally abused Cynthia and ended up emigrating to Canada with another woman. Although they had been separated for nearly thirteen years of their marriage, this wasn't a legal separation. When Cynthia finally got the courage to ask Joe for a divorce because she wanted to start her life over, Joe agreed but told her he wouldn't pay any maintenance. Cynthia hadn't received a dime from her deadbeat husband at any point in their marriage, so she didn't care—she just wanted to be legally single. Because the couple had few assets and no children, Cynthia went to court without any representation. And guess what she got: absolutely nothing except a piece of paper declaring her marriage dissolved. Yes, she simply wanted her

---

[9] Holland, Kelley. "We Know Why You and Your Spouse Will Fight Tonight." CNBC. February 04, 2015. Accessed May 11, 2016.
http://www.cnbc.com/2015/02/04/money-is-the-leading-cause-of-stress-in-relationships.html
[10] "TD Bank Surveys and Research." TD Bank News, Press Releases, Media Relations, Media Room. June 2015. Accessed May 11, 2016.
https://mediaroom.tdbank.com/couplesoverview

freedom, but I'm confident Cynthia could have come out of the marriage with considerably more if she'd hired an attorney or some form of counsel.

For those of you like Janette or Cynthia, there are outstanding resources available to you such as The Lilac Tree and Women's Divorce Resource Center.[11] These non-profit organizations provide support, advocacy, resources, referral services, and so much more to women before, during, and after a divorce. I'm a huge fan of these groups, and frankly, I wish I had known about them when I was going through my own. I strongly encourage you to contact them if you're contemplating divorce.

Pre-Divorce Preparation

Before the words "I want a divorce" are spoken, be sure you play an active role in, or are at least aware of, the family's finances. This includes everything from salaries to assets to debts. Regardless of who brings home the bigger paycheck, it's important to begin protecting everything you've brought into and have contributed to the household. You want to ensure you have copies of all financial records and are well-informed about the household's current financial situation. The bulk of your divorce will focus on money, so it's critical you have records and accurate information to share with your attorney. If you and your partner have a prenuptial agreement, make sure you have a copy of it.

Your mission during this pre-divorce time is to gather as much information about your household's financial situation as possible. This includes copies of financial statements, tax returns, real estate records, stocks, bonds, annuities, retirement and pension plans, accrued vacation time, military benefits, and even social security if either or both of you are over sixty-five. When adding up the assets, be sure to include automobiles, furnishings, collections such as art, air miles, and even season sports tickets. And don't forget to gather

---

[11] http://thelilactree.org
http://www.womens-divorce.org

documentation of all debts, including credit card statements, tax bills, and promissory notes.

One item many women overlook during this chaotic time is insurance. If you're on your partner's health insurance policy, you immediately need to look at alternatives. Many company-sponsored insurance plans consider divorce a "qualifying life event," and as such, they often allow employees to obtain health insurance outside the open enrollment period. Although Obamacare currently doesn't consider divorce a "qualifying life event," you're eligible for Obamacare outside the enrollment period if you lose your current insurance benefits.

In addition to health benefits, it's important to check the beneficiary on all of your life insurance policies. Keep in mind that the beneficiary can be changed at any point, but the thing with insurance is that the person who *owns* the policy is the *keeper* of the beneficiary key. If a spouse owns the life insurance policy, they are the only person who can change the beneficiary. What this means is that if you die with your husband as beneficiary, he gets everything—even if you're divorced. And the important thing to remember is that regardless of what your will states, the beneficiary wins. This is why it's in your best interest to have all insurance policies in *your* name, if at all possible.

If your future ex-spouse doesn't have life insurance, disability insurance, or long-term care insurance, now is the time to put these in place. While this might seem an odd time to purchase insurance for your soon-to-be ex, these ensure your former partner won't be able to take you back to court to lower your maintenance due to, for example, poor health. Again, I urge you to be the owner of these policies.

The Whisper File

When I was in the process of my own divorce, I created what I call a *whisper file*. It's basically a file with all your important documents and financial contact information. For example, your whisper file should include a list of your safety deposit box locations, attorney phone numbers, insurance policy numbers, and all other vital financial information and documents. It's essentially the file you'd grab if you had to quickly leave the house.

I also suggest you make a formal "To Do" list because, let's face it, there's simply too much to remember and too much that can fall through the cracks during this stressful time. When making your "To Do" list, be sure to include deadlines so that you don't keep your attorney waiting for any documents.

Finally, once you've filed for divorce, I think it's wise to ask the judge for a small, separate bank account so you can continue to manage basic day-to-day expenses. Even if the majority of your assets have been frozen, having a separate bank account is going to be important. You might even want to ask the court to require monthly deposits until your divorce is final. If your spouse refuses, ask the judge to order temporary support. In addition, begin to build credit if you don't have any credit in your name. I've known too many women who had no credit or savings in their names. If this is you, then get to work!

I know this is going to be a difficult time for you, but trust me, it's important that you think of divorce as a business transaction. You're going to have plenty of time to reflect on the breakdown of your marriage. But right now, you have to stay focused on protecting yourself and, if applicable, your children. Getting through this is going to take strength and courage. I know you've got both.

It's Time to Talk to Attorneys

Now that you have a firm grasp on the finances, it's time to consult an attorney. I've found that this is probably the hardest part of divorce for many women. Contacting an attorney makes the situation real. For some reason, talking to your family and friends about the divorce is totally different from discussing it with an attorney. If you were wishy-washy about seeing divorce as a business transaction, your attorney will confirm for you that it is indeed ALL about business. Right now is when it's crucial that you *listen* to your attorney. Yes, it's going to be a difficult conversation, and yes, your attorney will probably make it sound as if your spouse doesn't care about you and your children, but hear me out.

Think of your attorney as sort of a bodyguard. She's there to protect you.

Let her.

Of all the times in your life when you need an advocate—it's *now*. Don't let emotions get in the way. Remember, this is a *business* transaction. Harsh as that sounds, it's the way you need to think about this entire ordeal.

Choosing an Attorney

While we're on the subject of attorneys, let's discuss the process of obtaining one. You're about to go through a very difficult and emotional experience, so it's important that you interview several attorneys before making a decision. Ask for recommendations from friends and divorce advocacy organizations, look at reviews and ratings on the internet, and peruse attorney websites. In other words, do your research. Keep in mind that in certain states, legal fees can be absorbed by the one spouse that can afford them; thus, the spouse that cannot afford legal fees can have them paid in part or whole by the other spouse. This is called "leveling the playing field," and it allows for a spouse of lesser means to be legally represented in a manner comparable to the other party. There are caveats to this, so be sure to ask your attorney or another knowledgeable individual if this is something you should pursue.

You're looking for a really solid family law attorney who will fight for you and your children. I urge you not to settle for the first lawyer you speak with. Shop around until you find a combination of advocate and *shark*. You want someone who will fight for you and be as menacing as Jaws. I recommend you speak with the different attorneys on the phone to get information about their experience and specialties. Once you know the ones you'd like to interview, request a consultation to discuss your case.

And speaking of frightening, let me be the first to warn you that it's incredibly easy to be intimidated by a divorce attorney. Hey, they're supposed to be a little scary—that's what they're paid to do. However, remember that YOU are the client. Don't ever hesitate to ask questions or tell your lawyer to put what she said into layman's terms. And by all means, don't you dare agree to something you don't understand. Remember: this divorce can impact not just *your* future, but also your children's future. Pull up your big-girl pants and ask questions!

Conflicting Out

One last thing before we move away from the whole choosing-an-attorney discussion. I'm not necessarily suggesting you do the following, but I want to make sure you're aware of something called "conflicting out" attorneys. This sometimes happens in high-profile divorces or those where considerable assets are at stake. "Conflicting out" entails the sharing of confidential information with a potential attorney, thus making that attorney bound by the attorney-client privilege—and so unavailable to the opposing party in a case. As a result, if you share confidential information with an attorney, even if you choose not to hire them, your spouse will be unable to hire this attorney. It's an easy way to ensure your partner doesn't get the best divorce attorney in town, even if you can't afford to hire her.

Although you might think you'd never consider doing this, keep in mind that divorce can get ugly—never underestimate what your future ex-spouse might do. Don't wait too long to talk to attorneys.

Divorce is a Business Transaction

After you choose and hire an attorney, be prepared to begin feeling the impact of your decision. There will be a boatload of paperwork and choices regarding finances, the children, and assets. None of this is going to be easy for you, but I remind you once again to adopt the mantra, *"This is a business transaction."* Do not under any circumstances allow yourself to fall into an emotional sinkhole.

Your goal throughout the entire process is to protect you and your children. When your attorney asks about your children's college education funding, don't assume your soon-to-be-ex will contribute to their tuition. Make sure this is included in your divorce decree. Same thing for weddings. Yes, your former spouse might *tell* you not to worry about these expenses, but if it's not in the decree, there's no guarantee it'll be covered.

Margaret's Story

A dear friend of mine, "Margaret," went through an amicable divorce ten years ago. She and her ex, "Steven," had three beautiful daughters whom they both doted on. Steven assured Margaret that he would pay for college and give all three daughters lavish weddings. Because the couple had remained close even after the divorce, Margaret never once doubted Steven's intentions.

However, five years following the divorce, Steven remarried and started a family with his new wife. It wasn't long before Steven began to spend less time with his daughters from his first marriage. When the eldest told him about her plans to attend Vassar College, an out-of-state school, Steven informed Margaret that he could only contribute a small portion toward the tuition. A battle ensued that destroyed Steven's relationship with Margaret and his daughters forever. In the end, Steven didn't pay for anything that wasn't in the divorce decree. In other words—he paid NOTHING toward his children's college tuition. The girls had to take out student loans while Margaret frantically started saving money for her daughters' future.

Make sure that *everything* you want and need—now and in the future—is included in your divorce decree. Don't rely on promises from your former spouse or just assume he or she will take care of things. If it isn't in the decree, your ex-spouse doesn't have to pay for or do it. Period.

A divorce decree, or Decree of Dissolution of Marriage, is the final blueprint of the divorce. It tells you and your spouse exactly what is expected post-divorce. And let me tell you, the decree might as well be written in stone, because to change it requires piles of money for lawyer's fees, and even with the best attorneys on your side, there's only a slim chance of it being modified. This is why I suggest having it reviewed by at least two or three different attorneys before you sign it. Your signature on that document is the equivalent of the fat lady singing. Once you've signed the decree, it's over.

Read Your Future Spouse's Divorce Decree—Before You Get Remarried

Just as the divorce decree is critical when finalizing your divorce, it's equally important should you remarry at some point. If you plan to marry someone who has been divorced, it's absolutely vital that you read their divorce decree. The decree is a legal document that can dramatically affect your future happiness with your beloved.

Because a divorce decree is a legal document, it's a road map for the new spouse so that she's aware of what she's getting herself into financially. It lets her know if her future spouse is free and clear or if she'll be dealing with the legal equivalent of the proverbial albatross. I refer to the decree this way because, as I've mentioned above, once a divorce decree has been signed by both parties it is very costly and difficult to make changes to it. Consequently, if it's already a burden for your potential new spouse, it could very well end up being one for you, too.

Diane's Story

Let me tell you about "Diane," a client who came to me in tears about her recent marriage. After having been alone for a number of years, Diane was thrilled to meet and fall in love with her Prince Charming. She was swept away by his posh house and sleek car. She couldn't believe her luck, not just in meeting such a successful man, but one who loved her as much as she loved him.

Even though Diane had experienced love and loss—this was her second marriage—she never once thought about her new husband's previous marriage.

So, standing in front of me was this incredibly smart and

financially savvy woman who was seriously distraught because she had just discovered that her new husband's divorce decree called for, among other provisions, an exorbitant monthly alimony payment to his ex-wife.

Diane couldn't believe that she hadn't read the decree before she said "I do." She showed me the list of provisions her Prince Charming had promised his ex-wife. As I scanned the items in the decree—I won't lie—I was stunned. Her new husband had basically guaranteed his ex-wife a princess lifestyle for the rest of her days. I'm not just talking about a substantial amount of money and a house, but a new leased car every three years, gas money, a monthly clothing allowance, medical expenses, and even two annual vacations abroad.

I immediately sent Diane to a lawyer to see if the decree could be modified. Much to Diane's dismay, her attorney warned her not to expect too much relief from the post-decree petition, because unless minor children are involved, it is nearly impossible to get a divorce decree changed. The court requires the party requesting the modification to prove that there has been a "substantial change of circumstances." Diane's attorney wasn't confident that he could make a solid case. He reminded her that when you marry someone who has been divorced, you also marry that person's divorce decree.

In other words, Diane and her new husband would be financially supporting his ex-wife until she died.

Trust me, Diane isn't alone. Many soon-to-be-remarried couples are completely oblivious to their new partner's divorce decree. I understand how exciting it is to rediscover love, but you have to protect yourself. If your future partner has gone through a divorce, make sure you read the decree before you walk down the aisle.

Jill's Story

"Jill's" family suffered because of her husband's divorce decree. Jill married a man who had been divorced for almost five years before they met. As Jill would tell it, she and her husband fell in love instantly. It was a combination of the twinkle in her husband's deep blue eyes and his handsome good looks—it was love at first sight. After a whirlwind romance, the two married. However, it wasn't until quite a while after they were married that they discussed finances. This was when Jill discovered that her new husband was responsible for monthly maintenance and child support payments. Her two stepchildren were young, so Jill knew that the child support would be a long-term financial burden. To add to their financial woes, Jill found a provision in the divorce decree that her husband would also pay for the children's college education.

While this added expense might not have hurt some families, Jill was a stay-at-home mom to a newborn son and pregnant with another child. Her husband was the sole earner for the household. Every penny counted to this family as they constantly struggled to make ends meet.

As the years passed, Jill's family grew. Soon she had three children approaching college age. Unfortunately, the family had little savings, and the couple couldn't provide their children with money for college. One child chose to enter the military in order to obtain the college education benefits. Another child worked extremely hard in high school and obtained scholarships for his education. Their youngest child decided to forgo college altogether.

Although Jill rarely expressed resentment about her financial situation, it was obvious that she was eager for her husband's financial responsibility to his ex-wife and children to end. It was clear that the additional expense had prevented her family from doing many things they wished they could have done.

I have no doubt that Jill would have married her husband regardless of his divorce decree, but it's important to know what baggage your future partner is bringing to the relationship. Nobody wants a surprise like Jill's or Diane's.

Make the Best of Your Odds

Let's face it, marriage can be difficult. After all, nearly 50 percent of all marriages end in divorce. Scary statistics, right? Well, that's nothing when you consider that 60-67 percent of second marriages and 70-73 percent of third marriages fail. If you're marrying someone who is divorced, the odds are already against you.

There are many theories as to why this is the case.[12] Some think that people remarry too quickly, before having processed their previous failed relationships. Others hypothesize that once you've been through one divorce you "know the ropes" of the process and are not as afraid to move on once you realize a relationship is not working. However, it's very likely that finances play a major role in most divorces, regardless of other causes, whether it's the first, second, third or . . . Well, you get the picture.

So how can you help put the odds back in your favor?

Know what you're signing on for when you finalize your own divorce. And know what your new partner's obligations are to any previous relationships—before you walk back down that aisle!

---

[12] Banschick, Mark. "The High Failure Rate of Second and Third Marriages." Psychology Today. February 6, 2012. Accessed May 11, 2016. https://www.psychologytoday.com/blog/the-intelligent-divorce/201202/the-high -failure-rate-second-and-third-marriages

Financial Questions to Ask Before, During, and After Getting Divorced

Finances

1. What is the state of the family's finances? Where are copies of financial materials, such as bank and credit card statements, real estate deeds, automobile titles, etc.? Is everything in one place?

2. If assets are frozen, can I open a separate personal checking account in order to manage day-to-day expenses? Can I request a monthly deposit from my spouse, if necessary?

Attorneys

3. What will it cost to work with you? What is your strategy?

4. How will the assets and debts be divided?

5. How will custody of children be divided?

6. Who gets custody of the family pets?

Divorce Decree

7. Is everything I've requested in the decree? (If not, do NOT sign it until it's complete!)

8. Have I had the decree read by a different attorney?

Remarriage: Divorce Decree

9. Have I read my future partner's divorce decree BEFORE getting married?

10. Do I understand my future partner's financial obligations to his former family?

Let's Hear from the Experts

Victoria Sushan

Victoria Sushan is a Certified Divorce Financial Analyst, Financial Advisor, Divorce Mediator, and Collaborative Divorce Practitioner. She has been serving clients for over twenty years.

Marriage is about love and divorce is about money! My goal is to educate and motivate you to avoid the financial pitfalls of divorce. I believe that everyone is entitled to financial dignity during and after a divorce, and the best way to achieve this is to have the knowledge and information to make sound decisions.

Below are lists to help guide you through the divorce process:

TAKE STOCK OF EVERYTHING YOU HAVE

- Know your mortgage company for any primary residence and investment property, as well as your loan number, payment amount, interest rate, and escrow account.
- Compile statements for checking and savings accounts for the last five years.
- Compile tax returns for the last five years.
- Collect statements for stocks, 401(k) and IRA accounts, pension plans, and any profit-sharing accounts, including details of any loans taken against them and future benefit statements.
- Collect documents related to ownership in any businesses.
- Collect Social Security statements for current or future benefit payments.
- Verify and collect any credit card statements, including joint or individual.
- Verify and gather statements regarding any personal loans, student loans, or lines of credit.
- Provide information on any significant cash transactions that you and your partner have made. These include any major purchases that you've paid cash for without receipts.

- Collect information on any life insurance policies.
- Take a household inventory.

BE PROACTIVE

- Protect your valuables; for example, put your jewelry in a safety deposit box.
- Track your expenses.
- Organize your financial records.
- Review your will and/or estate plan.
- Obtain a credit report on the other spouse.

LEARN ABOUT DIVORCE OPTIONS AVAILABLE TO YOU

- Consult with a Certified Divorce Financial Analyst (CDFA) in your area. The role of the CDFA is to help you understand how the financial decisions you make today will impact your financial future.
- Research collaborative divorce and divorce mediation processes. This will save you time and money as you embark on the "divorce journey."
- Make smart financial decisions—not emotional ones.

HOW TO MAINTAIN POSITIVE CASH FLOW

- Find out what money sources are available to you before, during, and after the divorce. This includes income from any earnings, marital and individual assets, child support, and/or spousal support.
- Develop a pre-divorce and post-divorce budget. You can work on this with your CDFA or financial planner.
- All assets are not created equal, so it's important you understand what is considered separate and marital property in the divorce. Your attorney or your CDFA can educate you on this.
- Marital Home: the question is to sell or keep it.
- Address how the bills will be paid during the divorce.

UNDERSTAND THE KEY PLAYERS IN
YOUR DIVORCE PROCESS

- The divorce process you choose—litigation, mediation, or collaborative—will have a huge impact on the cost of this expensive vacation called "divorce." Mediation and collaborative processes allow you more control of the process and regulate how your money will be spent.
- You might need to hire additional experts, such as appraisers, business valuators, and perhaps a court-appointed child expert.

Alan Pearlman

Alan Pearlman is a Family Law attorney who has been serving the Chicago area for over forty years. He is also a member of several Bar Association Groups and teaches in his area of practice, as well as in the area of Legal Technology.

You must always remember that divorce, just like a business partnership that has gone askew, is just that: the breaking up of a partnership. This will cause a division of assets, debt, and other items that the business acquired during its years together. Throughout my forty years as a family law attorney, I have observed five common mistakes made while contemplating and going through a divorce.

Although there are many reasons why marriages end, infidelity is one of the leading causes.[13] This brings us to our first mistake: lack of observation. It's important to watch your spouse. Has he or she always come home for the past ten years at 5:30 or 6:00 p.m. but is now suddenly working more hours and coming home late? Are bills that normally went to your home address now not in the mail box? These may all be telltale signs of a paramour lurking in the background. And often, the reaction is to become indignant and

---

[13] "Divorce in America: Who Wants Out and Why? | Austin Institute." Austin Institute for the Study of Family and Culture. April 9, 2014. Accessed May 11, 2016. http://www.austin-institute.org/research/divorce-in-america/

confront their partner. Instead, you need to pay attention to what's going on around you and start thinking about what you can do to prepare yourself and to plan. This takes us to the second mistake I often see being made.

Mistake number two is not giving yourself enough time to plan and know all that there is to know about your fiscal partnership. Before you even broach the subject of a divorce, make sure you have copies of all tax returns for the last five years, copies of all check registries, copies of all stocks, bonds, IRAs, 401(k)s and so on. When you seek legal counsel, you're going to need to have access to as much of the partnership's financial information as is humanly possible.

Mistake number three is not having sufficient funds to hire competent legal counsel. Most professionals charge in accordance with their experience and length of service in the profession. Many potential clients may say to them, "You're really expensive and out of my price range." The response to this type of comment is simple: If you hire someone with less experience, you'll find yourself paying even more. Remember the old adage, "If you think it's expensive to hire a professional to do the job, wait until you hire an amateur."[14]

Take the time before contemplating divorce to save money any way you can. The more you save in the beginning, the better your plan will become. If there isn't any extra money to spare, ask a friend or relative to loan you the funds, but do this *before* you divulge your plans to your spouse. You don't want to risk not having time to accumulate the funds necessary to retain an experienced attorney.

Mistake number four is associated with number three. Simply stated, many folks will go to an attorney and say, "I can't afford to get divorced." They're often under the assumption that they can ask the court to do something about "leveling the playing field" by obtaining funds for attorney's fees from their spouse. This is only a half truth. Consider where that money is ultimately coming from.

---

[14] Red Adair. See: "Red Adair." Wikipedia. Accessed May 11, 2016. https://en.wikipedia.org/wiki/Red_Adair

Think of it this way: your marital assets—everything you and your spouse have accumulated during the marriage—is known as the *marital estate*. When a court awards attorney's fees to one or the other party, the money is actually just an advance against the portion of the marital estate that individual will receive upon dissolution of the marriage. In other words, if you ask for and receive an award for attorney's fees, you're essentially paying those fees yourself; the money is coming to you as an advance against whatever your final portion of the marital estate will be. So don't do this unless you absolutely have to. After all, you're going to need as much money as possible to start your new life. So start saving for attorney's fees well in advance of beginning divorce proceedings.

Finally, we come to mistake number five. The common thread here has been planning, or the lack thereof. When most people think of divorce planning, it's usually in terms of attorneys and court. However, you need other top professionals to help you through this legal maze. Most importantly, prior to filing your case, speak with and obtain the advice and counsel of a solid financial planner. Take the time to sit down and have that heart-to-heart talk about just exactly what needs to be done. After the divorce is over, it's too late. Items and assets will have changed hands, and rulings will become final. Prior to this, you and your financial planner can arrange the best possible outcome for you to begin rebuilding your new life. Also, a solid financial planner will work hand-in-hand with your attorney to work out how to accomplish these goals.

The key is to plan, plan, and then plan some more. Don't jump in the ocean if you can't swim. Likewise, don't confront your spouse before you have everything in place and are ready for action.

Wrap-Up

Why You Need to Talk about Divorce

1. Divorce is a highly emotional process, but your primary job throughout the entire ordeal is to protect yourself and your children. Therefore, your mantra *must* be "This is a business transaction."

2. Get your finances in order. This includes creating a *whisper file*—a file with all of your financial contact information and important financial documents. In addition, create a "To Do" list to track what you've given to your attorney and what needs to be sent.

3. Ensure you're the owner of your life insurance policy. If possible, be the owner of all insurance policies for you and your soon-to-be-ex spouse before you divorce. This includes life, disability, and long-term care insurance. You don't want to risk a trip back to court due to your ex's inability to make maintenance or child support payments because of illness or disability.

4. Request to open a small, separate checking account for day-to-day expenses after filing for divorce. Ask the judge for a monthly deposit until your divorce is finalized.

5. Make a complete list of assets and income. This can include everything from life insurance policies to social security. Be thorough!

6. Interview at least three different divorce/family law attorneys before choosing one.

7. Don't be intimidated by your attorney. Ask questions and NEVER agree to anything unless you completely understand it.

8. Talk to attorneys as soon as you've decided to file for divorce. Don't allow your partner to "conflict out" the top attorneys in your city.

9. A divorce decree, or Decree of Dissolution of Marriage, is a legal document that is very difficult to modify. Get a second or even third opinion on your decree from different attorneys before you sign it.

10. Don't forget to include future events, such as your children's college education, weddings, trust funds, etc., before you sign the divorce decree. Your former spouse is *only* legally bound to do what's in the divorce decree—nothing more, even if they promise at the time of the divorce that they'll do something in the future. Ask for it to be put in the decree before you sign it!

11. Be sure to read your future partner's decree BEFORE you get married! A divorce decree can create family tension and resentment in future nuptials. Second marriages have their own set of challenges, but adding in a financial commitment to a former spouse only makes those first years of married life even more difficult.

Let's Talk about Work

*The real money you lose in life is the
money you fail to earn.*

Chellie Campbell

Chapter 4

You Gotta Know When to Hold 'Em and Know When to Fold 'Em: The Secrets of Getting and Leaving a Job

Y ou've finally gotten an interview with the company of your dreams. The interview is going great as you elaborate on your accomplishments, and then you're asked about your salary requirements. You confidently respond, "My salary is negotiable." After a little small talk, the interview ends, you shake hands and thank the team of interviewers, and then walk out of the office. Giddy with excitement at how well your interview went, you phone your best friend while leaving the building and hope you hear back with an offer later in the week. Sounds great, right?

Think again.

Just Say "No"

Here's the problem with saying your salary is "negotiable": most women don't actually *negotiate*.

What we do is *accept the first offer*.

Trust me, I know all too well the exhilaration of receiving and accepting an offer for the job of your dreams. When I first started in the financial industry, I was so grateful to get the job that negotiating for a higher wage wasn't even a consideration. It wasn't until I started working that I discovered I was making considerably less than the men in my department who had started at the same time as me and who were doing the same job. And even *with* this knowledge, I didn't want to rock the boat and risk being viewed as unlikeable.

The Gender Pay Gap in Action

Want to know just how bad the situation is? In 2014, an Australian tech exec and former Victorian MP, Evan Thornley, went on record saying that he was able to hire talented women "relatively cheap" compared to men because of the gender pay gap.[15] Thornley actually bragged about this at a technology start-up conference and went on to say that although he considered this "opportunistic," he felt it was "an opportunity for forward thinking people." To make his point sting even stronger, Thornley showed a meme stating, "Women—like men, only cheaper."

Well here's the deal: if our silence continues, we *might* eventually earn the same amount as men—by 2133.[16]

I don't know about you, but I'm not willing to wait. As it is, the United States ranks 74th out of 145 countries for wage equality.[17] Looking at the data, the gender pay gap is actually getting *worse*! I think it's time we finally do something about this, and thankfully, I'm not alone. Most prominent business schools teach job negotiation classes. Some even require MBA grads to refuse their first job offer. Harvard Business School offers a four-day seminar for non-students focused on nothing but business negotiation skills. The Boston Office of Women's Advancement (OWA)[18] offers free job negotiation training to local women who work in the city. In fact,

---

[15] Covert, Bryce. "Tech Executive Brags He Was Able To Hire Talented Women 'Relatively Cheap' Compared To Men." ThinkProgress RSS. September 26, 2014. Accessed May 11, 2016.
http://thinkprogress.org/economy/2014/09/26/3572572/tech-exec-gender-wage-gap/

[16] Kottasova, Ivana. "U.S. Gender Pay Gap Is Getting Worse." CNNMoney. November 18, 2015. Accessed May 11, 2016.
http://money.cnn.com/2015/11/18/news/gender-pay-gap/

[17] *Ibid.*

[18] Cityofboston.gov - Official Web Site of the City of Boston. Office of Women's Advancement. Accessed May 11, 2016.
http://www.cityofboston.gov/women/

the OWA plans to expand the training to other major U.S. cities.

Negotiating isn't a skill you're born with. It's one that is learned, practiced, and honed.

Now About that Offer . . .

So, let's say you've received an offer from your dream company. Hopefully you had an idea of the offer you were anticipating *before* you interviewed. This is why it's important to do your homework first. Research, research, research. Before you arrive for your interview, you should have studied the company's website. I'm not saying you have to memorize the staff directory, but you should have a really good idea of what the company does, who their key players are, and where you would fit into their team. Look at their published annual reports, read press releases, and review any other data you can find on the internet. This isn't a dress rehearsal, folks, this is the real thing. Be prepared to dazzle them with your vast knowledge about the company—including salaries.

Know Your Market Value

Before you enter your prospective employer's building, know your market value and the salary range of the position for which you're interviewing. There are loads of resources on the internet to help you figure this out, such as Salary Expert, Salary.com, and many others. These sites offer salary information for most jobs in nearly all geographic locations. In addition, they factor in the cost of living. This is especially important if you're looking to relocate. The last thing you want is to find yourself with an offer in a city you can't afford. If you're planning to make a major move, be sure to factor in these costs as you explore the salary range for your desired job. Another way to determine an appropriate salary is to look at postings for jobs at companies within your industry. Most ads include salary specifications.

During the interview, you might be asked the trap question: "What are you making at your current job?" The fact is, a new job offer shouldn't be based on your previous or present employment. It should reflect the amount of work and skills needed for the *new* job, as well as what you're bringing into the company. Again, this is where your research comes in handy. Hedge this question by telling the interviewer the salary range that you're seeking. Don't be afraid to speak up and tell your potential employer what you're worth. Yes, you will most likely have to negotiate, but don't lowball your value. It's much harder to increase your salary after you've accepted the offer. If you don't ask for what you're worth, who will do this for you?

I have a client, "Anna," who is a university professor. When Anna first accepted her tenure-track position, she was so elated to get the offer that she didn't think she could negotiate for more money. Instead, she requested a university laptop and a semester off to finish her dissertation. As a result, Anna began her job at the bottom of the pay scale. It wasn't until Anna received a substantial offer from another university two years later that she was able to negotiate for more pay. This experience taught Anna a very valuable and costly lesson.

Let's Talk about Benefits

Another mistake I've seen women make is not really exploring the benefits package of a potential employer. Chances are you'll be offered insurance, paid time off, retirement, and other forms of compensation. Because these tend to be the norm for a salaried position, many people skim over the paperwork and focus only on the salary.

Don't do this! The offered benefits package can make the salary more significant—or it can reduce the impact of the dollar signs. What I'm suggesting is this: it might seem like you're being offered more money than the average expected salary for a comparable position. But if you're receiving less paid time off and fewer sick days, you won't really be earning more.

And it's not just your vacation time you should consider. Some companies pay the full price for employee insurance. However, many businesses now require individuals to contribute a portion of the amount. You need to factor these costs into your salary. The benefits package is really important to any job offer. Again, I encourage you to do some research before your interview. Find out what comparable companies are offering their employees in terms of health insurance, paid leave, retirement plans, and other perks. Then factor in these costs and benefits when evaluating your salary offer.

Negotiating for a Benefits Package

There are other potential benefits to consider. You could, for example, consider negotiating for the ability to work from home. As you probably already know, child care is extremely expensive. I've worked with many clients who eventually quit their jobs not because they necessarily wanted to be stay-at-home moms, but rather because they were working to pay for child care. My client, "Stephanie," and I worked out that after taxes it was actually cheaper for her to stay home than to send her newborn twins to day care. Based on this information, Stephanie decided to talk to her supervisor to see if it was possible to work from home three days a week. Because she was a valued employee, Stephanie's boss agreed to the arrangement. Stephanie hired a babysitter twice a week for the days she had to go to the office, and also had the sitter help with the twins occasionally during the days Stephanie was home. The cost savings was substantial, and Stephanie essentially had the best of both worlds.

Many employers are now offering women and family-friendly benefits, such as the ability to leave work to care for a sick child, paid maternity leave, and onsite nursing stations and child care facilities. Other benefits you might look for include an on-site gym or a subsidy for a local health club, a wardrobe allowance, transportation reimbursement, relocation assistance, education reimbursement, and a company cell phone. Keep in mind that these extras could impact your taxes, so it's advisable to consult a tax advisor.

One of my favorite perks that many employers throw out to their prospective employees is a company car. While this benefit is definitely enticing, it's important to read the fine print. A young client of mine, "Meg," accepted her first job in Columbus, Ohio after graduation. Having grown up in New York City and relying on public transportation her entire life, Meg's new employer lured her in with the promise of a company car. Meg excitedly learned how to drive, got her license, and was busy shopping for cars when she realized that her employer's idea of a "company car" was merely compensation for a car payment. In other words, Meg received a monthly bonus of $300 in lieu of an actual vehicle. Meg hadn't read the contract closely, and it wasn't until she had already relocated for the job that she made this discovery. Not only was Meg being taxed on the amount her company allocated for the car payment, but she was also expected to pay vehicle taxes and license plate fees from her monthly stipend. The moral to Meg's sad story is this: read the contract . . . and then read it again. Your future employer can offer you a plethora of goodies, but if they're not spelled out in the contract, you might not get what you think you've been promised.

Go Prepared

Go into the interview knowing what benefits you need. Of course, don't go all diva on your future employer and make ludicrous demands, but be sensible and stand up for what you really desire. Yes, you want to be likeable during negotiations, but you also need to be firm. Don't be afraid to say "no." I know, "no" is not a word many of us frequently use, but in the case of job negotiations, it's important you learn how to say it. Don't be aggressive or shout it out, but be secure and stay true to your wishes. This is business, not personal.

Think of it like shopping for a new car. A savvy buyer isn't going to accept the first price the salesperson tosses out. Same thing with your job offer. Study the offer closely to ensure it's a fair proposal and to determine if there's anything you'd like to add. I can't say it enough: don't wait to negotiate until you're hired! Once you're on the payroll, it's much more difficult to obtain a higher salary and increased benefits. Strike while the iron is hot!

It's Never Too Late to Ask

Okay, well let's say you're already in your dream job, but alas, you didn't negotiate for your salary or benefits. You're not alone. I've spoken to countless women who are in your same shoes, and as I told you at the beginning of the chapter, I was one of them. Although it's not easy to negotiate once you have the job, there are definitely some strategies you can use to open the conversation.

We've all worked in an office with at least one or two disgruntled employees. These people are toxic to the work environment and employee morale. Don't become one of them if you find yourself discouraged and feel as if you're underpaid. Speak to your supervisor about your issues before you fall prey to bitterness.

Prior to making an appointment with your boss, prepare a solid case for a raise or additional benefits. The first thing to do is shop your industry's competitors. Just as when you're initially negotiating for a job, you need to know your market value. If you're a yoga teacher, find out what other yoga studios are offering teachers with your experience.

I also suggest you quantify as best you can things like the amount of new business you've brought to the company, expenses you've saved, cost-saving systems you've initiated . . . you get the picture. In other words, toot your horn, and then toot it again! This is the perfect opportunity to pull out your previous performance reviews while you make a list of what you've done to boost your company's value. Show your boss how lucky the company is to have an employee like you. I have a friend, "Trina," who saved her company thousands of dollars every year simply because she changed office supply vendors. Trina's supervisor had used the same supplier for over a decade, but when Trina sought a competitive bid from another vendor and convinced her boss to switch, the company's office supply costs were cut in half.

When working on your list of what you provide to the company, don't forget to mention all the extras you do. If you bring in bagels on Fridays, make coffee in the morning, greet customers and make them feel welcome, or help colleagues when they're falling behind, be sure to bring this up when you meet with your supervisor. Companies not only hate to lose productive employees, they also hate to lose employees who create a positive work environment.

Don't be shy—tell your company exactly how much you've saved them and/or how much you've brought in. I know, as women we're notorious for hiding in the shadows and being humble about our successes. Well, if there's one thing I've learned in my lifetime, it's that if we don't brag about our accomplishments, we're more likely to be taken advantage of.

So start talking!

Calling it Quits

Is it your secret fantasy to walk into your boss's office, hand over your resignation and then tell your boss exactly how you feel about him or her? C'mon, fess up! We've all been there at some point in our career. But even if you have the perfect new job lined up, depending on how long you've worked for your current company, this might not be the ideal strategy for your bank account or future retirement. There are several things you'll want to consider before calling it quits.

First off, make sure you've really considered *why* you're leaving your job. Regardless of the reason, discuss it with your boss. Companies usually want valued team players, and if you're leaving for more money, be sure this is known before you walk out the door. It's even more important to talk to your supervisor or HR if it's a work-related issue—that is, if there's a problem with another employee, working conditions, or anything else. I've known too many people who have quit their jobs only to find themselves without an income for several months. If they'd only had the chutzpah to address problematic conditions while still on the job, they might still be employed.

That said, if you feel you just can't take it anymore and you plan to quit—no matter what!—you'll want to make sure ahead of time that you're prepared both financially and professionally.

For example, you won't be eligible for unemployment benefits if you quit your job, so you'll need to have sufficient funds stockpiled in the event you can't find a new job for at least six months. Make sure your resume is current and your networking social media, such as LinkedIn, is updated. Keep a cautious eye on the job market. And take stock of what you'll leave behind at your current job, such as health and life insurance, as well as retirement benefits.

For example, although only about 25 percent of Fortune 500 companies currently offer an employee retirement plan (profit-sharing or pension),[19] many public jobs still come with this gold-plated retirement perk. Even if your employer offers a 401(k) option in lieu of a pension, it's still important to plan out what you'll do with your retirement funds if you quit. What's more, timing can be key when it comes to leaving a job with benefits, so it's important to address the benefits issues *before* you walk out that door.

Christina's Story

I worked with a client, "Christina," who had been with a prominent marketing agency in New York City for nine-and-a-half years. The mother of three school-aged children, Christina found it increasingly difficult to maintain her full-time work schedule after she divorced.

Although her employer hated the thought of Christina leaving, they understood her situation. They threw Christina a big farewell party and presented her with a $10,000 bonus check. Christina was elated. She hadn't been expecting such a generous bonus, and she knew the money would come in handy. Christina came to see me several months after leaving her job. She hadn't mentioned this life-changing decision in any of our previous meetings, so I was

---

[19] Marte, Jonnelle. "Nearly a Quarter of Fortune 500 Companies Still Offer Pensions to New Hires." Washington Post. September 5, 2014. Accessed May 11, 2016.
https://www.washingtonpost.com/news/get-there/wp/2014/09/05/nearly-a-quarter-of-fortune-500-companies-still-offer-pensions-to-new-hires/

stunned when she told me. Christina excitedly informed me that her company had given her the bonus, and she wanted to know how to invest it.

I hated to burst Christina's bubble, but I had no choice.

The "generous" bonus she had received was mere pennies compared to what she had given up by leaving her job before she had been vested in her company's retirement plan. That's right, Christina was only a few months away from securing her future. Other than giving her a summary plan, nobody in HR had advised her to stay just a little longer with the company. And of course, Christina had no idea she would be losing hundreds of thousands of dollars in retirement benefits.

Okay, don't get me wrong. I'm not blaming the folks in HR for not warning her by offering this critically important financial information. After all, they were simply doing their jobs. This is why it's important to remember that HR works for the company, not the employees. And let's face it, most companies, especially in corporate America, will do whatever possible to save a nickel. This is why you need to find out what you're potentially leaving behind—and how to make sure you take it with you.

Know What You're Leaving Behind

So let's talk about your profit-sharing, pension and/or 401(k) plans. Although these both achieve the same goal—money for retirement—they are very different animals. I explain the differences in greater detail in Chapter 10, but the short and sweet of it is this—your employer is responsible for making sound investments if you have a profit-sharing or pension plan, but if you have a 401(k), it's *your* job to make sure your money is invested wisely. Sounds simple, but of course, there are caveats to both.

Perhaps the most important word to add to your benefits vocabulary is vesting. And no, I'm not talking about clothing! Regardless of whether your company offers a profit-sharing, pension or 401(k), you will most likely have to become vested before you can receive employer-contributed retirement benefits.

This vesting time period varies depending on your employer's plan, but it can range from three to ten years. In addition to knowing your company's vesting period, it's also important to learn what type of vesting they have. There are two basic types of vesting: cliff (all or nothing) and graded (you receive a percentage based on the number of years). Unfortunately, Christina's marketing agency had a ten-year cliff vesting period. Because she left her job before the ten-year mark, Christina lost everything her employer had contributed.

What to Do with Your 401 (k)

Pension plans are in the hands of your employer, but if you have a 401(k) and want to leave your job, it's up to you to decide what to do with your nest egg. This isn't a terribly difficult dilemma because you really only have three choices—leave your 401(k) where it is, take it with you, or roll it over into a new plan. There are caveats and benefits to all three.

If your vested 401(k) balance is less than $5,000, your employer will most likely require you to withdraw it and invest elsewhere. Just remember that you will be taxed heavily on this amount, so before you go on a spending spree, be sure to check with your accountant or tax preparer.

I'm a strong advocate of taking your 401(k) with you. Your former employer usually prefers this option because they don't want to manage and hold your 401(k) funds. It costs them money, and because it's still with them, they have some responsibility for it. I suggest you either transfer your funds into another company's 401(k) plan or roll it into an IRA Rollover in your own name. Doing this defers income taxes on distribution when you reach retirement age. If you have multiple 401(k) accounts, you will need to be very diligent about keeping track of them to ensure that they're properly disbursed when it comes time to receive these funds. I talk more about this in Chapter 10, but the deal is this: fewer accounts equal fewer opportunities for mistakes to occur. I urge my clients to roll their money into an IRA Rollover so they can monitor their nest egg.

Hey, it's always easier to manage an account if it's all in one place. And when it's time to take income from your retirement account, or you reach the required minimum distribution age of 70½ years old, it will be much easier to do the calculations accurately. If you miss one account that is still at a previous employer or with a different financial institution, you can be penalized up to 50 percent by the IRS for not taking the required minimum distribution from that account.

There's another reason I favor IRA Rollovers. The average Baby Boomer will have held 11.7 jobs between the ages of 18-48.[20] Job-hopping Millennials are expected to have 15-20 jobs over the course of their lives.[21] You do the math. This is why keeping each 401(k) rolled over into one IRA Rollover with your name on it makes the most sense to me.

Whether your former employer allows you to keep your retirement money with the company or you transfer it into your new company's 401(k), be sure you keep records and know exactly where your money is located. I had a client who changed jobs frequently because her husband was a college professor and moved fairly often. As a result, "Jess," approached retirement not knowing anything about the retirement plans she had contributed to. I'm not kidding. Jess didn't know how much money she had invested, and even worse, she didn't know the names of the companies holding her money. It took some real sleuthing to get everything organized, but so much time could have been saved if Jess had kept good records of these funds and made sure the relevant employers had her forwarding address. Bottom line is this: take your retirement funds with you when you leave a company.

The other option for your 401(k) is to transfer funds into another

---

[20] "NLS FAQs." U.S. Bureau of Labor Statistics. Accessed May 11, 2016. http://www.bls.gov/nls/nlsfaqs.htm#anch41

[21] Meister, Jeanne. "Job Hopping Is the 'New Normal' for Millennials: Three Ways to Prevent a Human Resource Nightmare." Forbes. August 14, 2012. Accessed May 11, 2016. http://www.forbes.com/sites/jeannemeister/2012/08/14/job-hopping-is-the-new-normal-for-millennials-three-ways-to-prevent-a-human-resource-nightmare/

tax-deferred plan. This means you can put that money into a current IRA or open a new account. It also means that you can roll over ("convert") from one type of plan to another. If you opt to do this, I highly recommend you consult a financial advisor to assist with selecting the best plan for your retirement funds. I have many new clients walk in with absolutely no idea how their retirement money has been invested. One recent client, "Abby," presented me with her paperwork and simply wrote her company's name in the retirement portion. When asked if she had a pension or a 401(k), Abby shrugged and said she thought it was a 401(k) but honestly didn't know. I asked if she had ever been given any investment options. Trying hard to think of a time this might have happened, Abby eventually nodded and said that she was pretty sure she had been, but she couldn't tell me what they were.

Sure, we're not all quite so oblivious of our retirement plans, but even those of us who have played the market and know quite a lot about investments should still talk to an advisor before taking risks with that golden retirement egg. This is why I think it's important for you to consult with a professional before making a decision about your retirement money.

Will You Still Have Health Insurance?

Retirement benefits aren't the only things you risk losing when you leave your job. When you meet with HR for your final farewell, the focus is usually on health insurance. You should be entitled to continued health care coverage under COBRA (Consolidated Omnibus Budget Reconciliation Act). COBRA is expensive, so you may want to check other insurance options.

Something else to look out for: if you're on COBRA for even one month, you might be disqualified from applying for an Obamacare health care plan during the Special Enrollment Period. Keep in mind there is a time limit for choosing and staying on a COBRA plan. Your HR representative will tell you how long you have to make a decision on whether or not you want to continue your current health care coverage with COBRA. The clock starts ticking the day you leave, so don't procrastinate. In addition, COBRA is meant to be a temporary solution, so depending on your plan, you only have between 18-36 months of coverage, assuming you pay your bill every month. The bottom line is this: before you quit your job, check your options with a health insurance expert. This is a decision you don't want to make hastily and without up-to-date information.

Will You Still Have Life Insurance?

Before you get too wrapped up in trying to figure out your medical care needs, don't forget all of the other perks your employer provided. I can't begin to tell you how many of my clients quit their jobs only to discover months later that they no longer have life insurance. While this protection might not seem as important as health care, let me tell you: life insurance is one of life's (and death's) necessary evils. Whether you have a family to support or just want to ensure your loved ones can pay the undertaker, you need life insurance. Depending on your age and health, life insurance can be costly; in some cases, it can be nearly impossible to obtain.

Much like health insurance, if you're older and have certain health conditions, you might not be able to find a company willing to insure you. And even if you do, be prepared to pay a whopping amount for the privilege. Most times when you leave a company, you leave behind the life insurance. You *might* be allowed to continue your employer group life insurance. The benefit to this is that medical exams are often waived, and hopefully, you'll get a lower rate.

I recommend you have private life insurance prior to leaving your current job, so you're still covered if and when you make the decision to leave. The reason I suggest this is because the amount of life insurance your company offers is usually insufficient to fund your family in the event something happens to you. It's important to calculate how much insurance you need to provide for your family. Again, I think it's wise to speak with a life insurance professional to ensure your dependent's lives won't be dramatically impacted financially by your death.

The bottom line is this: leaving behind employer-covered benefits can be costly, so before you hand in your resignation, it's absolutely vital you consider what it's going to cost you to quit your current job.

Giving Notice

Let's take one last look at the ramifications of voluntarily leaving a job. Whether you're contemplating quitting your job because of the work environment, you've found a better opportunity, or for personal reasons, making the decision to leave is never easy.

When you *do* decide to leave, it's advisable to know and allow for your current company's notice period. Some businesses ask for two weeks while others require a month or more. Make sure you do your best to give your current employer this time. You want to leave your job on good footing. Yes, it might be tempting to tell your boss to shove it and storm out the door, but you'd regret it. Trust me on this. Even if you're sure you'll never ask for a letter of recommendation from your employer, at some point in your career, you may cross paths with your former colleagues. If you've left on bad terms, such a departure can make for some very awkward encounters.

So when you leave, do it humbly and quietly. Save the celebration until you're safely out the door.

Questions to Ask When You're Negotiating for a Job and Before You Leave One

Negotiating

1. How frequently will I have a performance and salary review? Explain the salary review process and the merit increase structure.

2. How soon after hiring will I be eligible for insurance benefits?

3. Will the company offer any student loan assistance or pay for continuing education?

4. What kind of retirement package is offered? What is the vesting period and type?

5. If necessary, will there be an opportunity to work from home?

6. Will the company reimburse me for relocation expenses? What do these include?

7. Will the company assist in the sale of my house? Is there a company contingency plan in the event I can't sell my house?

8. Does the company offer a company car or a car allowance?

9. Does the company provide an allowance for cellular phone, wardrobe, or other business expenses I must incur?

10. If things go well, what does the path look like for someone who is successful at their job and who wants to move up in the company? For example, what might I expect to be doing in one year, three years, and five years?

11. If possible, may I speak with current employees in order to get a feel for the company's culture, compensation and benefits?

Calling it Quits

12. What health insurance options do I have if I leave?

13. What is the deadline for choosing COBRA? How long can I stay with my COBRA plan?

14. Will I be allowed to switch from a COBRA plan to an Obamacare plan if I'm currently insured by a COBRA policy?

15. Can I continue on the company's life insurance policy? If not, what are my options?

16. What other forms of insurance do I currently have? Can I continue on these? If not, what are my options?

17. Am I vested in the company's retirement plan? If not, what is the vestment period?

18. What paperwork do I need in order to take my 401(k) with me?

19. Will you write a favorable recommendation for future employment?

Let's Hear from the Expert

Ken Richman

Ken Richman is a partner in the Chicago law firm of Burke, Warren, MacKay & Serritella.

What advice would you give to someone new to the negotiating process?

It's important to do your homework and inventory what really matters to you before you begin the negotiating process for a new job. Even though the prospective employer may have a "standard benefits package," one size doesn't necessarily fit all. While this package may be an appropriate starting point for negotiations, many employers will accommodate an employee's needs, especially if what she's asking for is consistent with the market and if the employee has a skill set that the employer really needs. By all means, be clear about what is important to you and what you can work around. Playing cards close to the vest might work in poker, but in employment contract negotiations it just aggravates employers and adds time and cost to the process.

Should I ask for time before responding to an offer?

Absolutely! Don't be too quick to accept, compromise, or reject a proposal. When an offer is made, ask for time to consider it before responding. No job that I know of has ever been lost because an applicant took an evening to think it over.

I've hit a roadblock in the negotiation process. What do I do?

Don't let the negotiation momentum stop. Simply say, "That's a real problem for me, but let's keep working through the other points and we can come back to this one later." If you aren't making progress with the person representing your prospective employer, ask if others in the organization can be included in the negotiations. Negotiations are a person-to-person process, and sometimes a new face adds a dynamic that can move things along, either by virtue of the new person's authority level, knowledge of relevant facts, or personality.

I've heard that leverage is important in negotiations. What exactly does this mean?

Leverage is indeed important when negotiating. However, leverage must be created out of facts. What this means is that you can use your strong employment history, other employment options, and unique skills or certifications you can offer the company. These are tools you can use to leverage the best possible deal. One word of caution is that if you use these tools, make sure you have the facts to back them up. Remember that the employer may not be able to change his/her position in response, so you don't want to be caught in a lie. For example, if you inform your potential boss that you have other good employment opportunities, be sure you actually have these competing offers.

Any final suggestions for negotiating a contract?

Always provide a reason for accepting or rejecting a proposal. For example, you might tell your prospective employer that you can accept the salary level even though it's below market value, but you would need more flexibility in your schedule in order to reduce child care expenses. Just as you should provide a reason for rejection, you should expect the same from your prospective employer. Negotiation involves give-and-take through mutual fact-finding. When a prospective employer rejects your proposal, you need to know why so you can respond appropriately and work to find common ground. It's not rude or offensive to ask why your counter-offer was rejected.

What's the number one mistake employees make when leaving a job?

Not having good, current information about the specific market conditions for jobs in the employee's category and of the employee's rights to post-employment benefits from the employer she's leaving.

What advice would you give someone contemplating leaving a job?

Be realistic about your options, be clear about your objectives, and make sure that your options and objectives match up. For example, if you are leaving a job to make more money, make sure the market for your qualifications and experience will command a higher salary. Conversely, if you are leaving a job to gain better work-life balance, don't get sidetracked by marginally higher salary offers.

Am I eligible for unemployment benefits if I voluntarily leave my job?

In most states, employees who voluntarily leave their jobs are not eligible for unemployment compensation benefits. However, some states recognize that benefits are payable to employees who are "constructively discharged" (i.e., the employer took actions that forced the employee to terminate); and some employers do not routinely contest ex-employee claims for unemployment benefits. It costs very little (no money and just a little time) to file an application for unemployment benefits, so it may be worthwhile to do so even if your chance of getting benefits is low. But don't falsify your benefit application form.

What are the pros and cons of leaving my job when it comes to seeking future employment?

Most prospective employers would rather interview and hire a new employee who is working elsewhere at the time. For this and a host of other good reasons, it's preferable to keep your old job until you find a new one, if possible.

My dad always told me never to burn bridges. What's the best way to amicably leave a job?

Most employers I know want honesty from their employees and don't want to be left in a service or production bind. Employees who offer reasonable advance notice (either for a precise time period or until the conclusion of a discrete project), recommend successors and/or offer to provide training, avoid criticizing the employer or its management (i.e., it's not you, it's me), and avoid breaching non-solicitation and confidentiality agreements have the best chance of keeping bridges intact.

Wrap-Up
Why You Need to Know When to Hold 'Em
and Know When to Fold 'Em

1. Telling a prospective employer that your salary is "negotiable" is code for "I don't know how much I'm worth." Do your homework BEFORE the interview so you know the salary range for comparable jobs and your current job market value. When you present the salary range that you're willing to accept, do so with the caveat that you request a six-month review.

2. Don't EVER tell a prospective employer your current salary. This is a strategy for low-balling you. Be prepared to give a solid response to questions regarding your salary requirements. You're not at the interview to swap jobs at the same pay scale.

3. Carefully review your benefits package. Know what benefits federal and state laws require your company to offer. Some companies will offer a higher salary with fewer benefits. Don't take any benefits for granted. If they're not mentioned during the negotiations, mention them. Strike while the iron is hot!

4. Request a copy of the company's personnel handbook. This will give you a peek at the culture of the organization and what is expected should you accept the job.

5. Make a list and inventory exactly what it is you need to accept the job offer. Be reasonable and realistic – no divas allowed. However, be upfront and open about what it is you want. Don't play games with the negotiating team. You'll just piss them off and possibly hit a roadblock.

6. Really read the contract. If a company car has been offered, make sure it's an actual vehicle instead of a stipend for a car payment. This goes for everything you've discussed during negotiations. If you requested the flexibility to work from home, ensure it's spelled out exactly how many days you're expected to be in the office.

7. Negotiating is a business transaction. Don't take rejection as a personal affront. Instead, ask why your counter-offer was refused so that you and the negotiating team can find common ground. Speak up, and don't be afraid to say "no."

8. Don't wait until you're hired to negotiate. It's much harder to increase your salary and ask for additional perks after you've signed a contract or come to an agreement. The time to negotiate is BEFORE you've signed on the dotted line.

9. If you didn't negotiate when you were hired, make sure your boss acknowledges the value you bring to the company. When asking for a raise or additional benefits, be prepared with a list of your accomplishments and what you've done to improve the company and the work environment. Toot your own horn . . . several times!

10. Find out what kind of retirement plan your current employer offers. Is it a profit-sharing, pension, or a 401(k) plan?

11. The vesting period for employers varies. Make sure you know what the time period is for your situation, and figure out how close you are to becoming vested. Also, find out if it's a cliff (all or nothing) or a graded (based on number of years) plan.

12. Don't just quit your job in a huff. Leave on good terms and give your employer sufficient notice. Do your best to ensure you'll be missed—and not the topic of office gossip.

13. Decide where you want to put your retirement money. You have the option of withdrawing it, transferring it, or rolling it over into a personal 401(k). Review the pros and cons of each and keep track of where your money is located. Also, know the tax ramifications of having more than one 401(k).

14. Talk to a health insurance specialist to determine which health care option is best for you. The COBRA plan is the one you're on with your current employer, but it will cost you a great deal of money and can possibly disqualify you from subsidized health care through Obamacare. Check out your options before you meet with HR.

15. Ask your current employer about continuing your life insurance policy. If this isn't an option, amp up your private plan to make up for the loss. Make sure you have enough life insurance to support your family in the event something happens to you.

16. Your employer provides many additional insurance perks, from accidental death to cancer coverage. If you currently carry these plans, look for alternatives prior to handing in your notice.

Chapter 5

Talk Taxes to Me: How to Keep More of Your Hard-Earned Cash

There any many things in life that are uncertain, but one thing is for sure: when you have a source of income, you're going to have to pay taxes. If you're like the majority of my newer clients, you're a bit intimidated by the whole tax process.

The fear of being audited and a lack of understanding about taxes often cause many women to procrastinate filing or, even worse, to blindly sign a tax return without knowing what's in it. As a result, many end up paying greater taxes, penalties, and interest than they might need to otherwise. And if they don't pay, liens and levies will be instituted.

Well, come close because I have a secret to tell you.

Shhh . . . don't tell anyone, but Uncle Sam is actually your friend—a sort of team player. I know, I know—it's a difficult concept to embrace, but I promise you'll see him in a whole new light by the end of this chapter.

The Cardinal Rule of Taxes

Okay, before I go all "tax talk" on you, I'm going to start with the cardinal rule of taxes.

Don't ever, Ever, EVER sign a tax return unless you have read and thoroughly understand it.

Let me put it this way: when you sign a tax return, you're telling Uncle Sam that everything in the document is true and accurate. Period. The Internal Revenue Service (IRS) doesn't care if you signed under duress or had consumed one too many glasses of wine when your partner handed you the papers. Your signature is on the document, so you're liable for its contents.

I can't tell you how many women I've worked with who have confided that they never looked at a tax return before signing it. This is not only naïve—it's also incredibly reckless.

Stephanie's Story

A client, "Stephanie," came to see me following her divorce. I was stunned when I heard the news that she and her husband of twenty-four years had split. It wasn't until I looked at Stephanie's financial information that I began to put the pieces together. Stephanie's husband, "Joe," had three businesses that he hadn't reported to the IRS for FIVE years. Every year when Joe filed taxes, he'd pretty much tell Stephanie to "sign here" and, not really wanting to be involved in the process, Stephanie signed. Because Stephanie was listed as co-owner of the businesses, she was an accessory to the tax fraud her husband had committed. This didn't just destroy their marriage, it also resulted in their filing for bankruptcy and having to pay an exorbitant amount in penalties and back taxes. In a nutshell, Stephanie went from living a charmed life to having nothing.

I've known women whose lives were completely destroyed because they blindly signed fraudulent tax returns. Promise me that you'll never belong to this group! I assure you, taxes aren't that scary or difficult. Yes, the tax laws frequently change, but there is one constant: you have to file a return every year. Rather than dread tax time, think of it as an opportunity to do an annual review of your income and expenses. Most importantly though, don't become intimidated by the process. File your taxes on time and read them thoroughly before you sign on the dotted line. And if your tax returns are complicated, hire an experienced tax preparer or CPA.

Know Your Tax Bracket

Now let's get down to business. You've accepted your dream job, and the first thing HR hands you is a form called a W-4. This piece of paper, filled with the tiniest text you'll ever see, basically tells payroll how much of your salary you want them to withhold for taxes. Sounds simple, right? Well, this little form is the source of many questions clients ask me. The goal in filling out the W-4 is to withhold enough to pay your taxes, but not enough to get an April windfall. After all, you don't want to give Uncle Sam a zero percent interest loan. In other words, you need to be aware of your tax bracket so you don't withhold too much for income taxes from your paycheck.

Yes, we're going to talk about the mysterious tax bracket. If you've ever worked with an accountant or tax person, you've probably heard this term. However, chances are you really don't know what it is and how it affects your income. If this is the case, you're not alone. The bottom line, though, is this: your tax bracket determines the rate at which your income will be taxed. For example, if you're a single filer in 2015 making between $9,226 and $37,450, your income will be taxed at a 10 percent rate for the first $9,225, and then at a 15 percent rate on the remaining amount. Make one penny more, and your highest taxable income jumps to 25 percent. In other words, the more money you make, the more taxes you pay on the highest amount.

This doesn't mean you'll lose money if you get a raise, but know that if your new bonus throws you into the next bracket, you'll pay higher taxes. So it's crucial to be aware of your income tax bracket before you ask for a raise or any other taxable stipend.

And here's the tricky part about tax brackets: they fluctuate. There's a complicated process the government uses to determine when and how to make changes to the system, but the bottom line is this: you need to know your income tax bracket in order to reduce your taxes.

One reason for this is that with proper tax planning and an understanding of your tax bracket, you can be aware of how to make changes in income and tax-deductible expenses work to your advantage (professionals refer to the process as "timing of transactions"). For example, if you know that the 28 percent bracket cuts off at a certain taxable income amount, you would want to defer or freeze income and/or accelerate expenses to keep your rate at 28 percent instead of creeping into the next bracket, which is 33 percent. This process is not as complicated as it sounds; managing your tax bracket isn't brain surgery. Start exploring the IRS website[22] to get information about the current year's tax brackets and, if you feel it would be helpful, consider consulting with a professional.

The W-4

Now that you know what tax bracket you're in, it's time to calculate the amount you want to withhold from every paycheck. If you've ever looked at (and been confused by) a W-4, it's easy to understand why so many people simply list their number of dependents. However, this isn't necessarily the best strategy. You could either end up owing Uncle Sam a whopping amount due to underpayment or offering him an interest-free loan. Neither option is good for your budget or bank account.

Yes, the W-4 looks daunting due to its fine print and formulas, but go online and you'll find a much easier and user-friendly way to determine the amount you need to withhold for taxes. The IRS offers several different tools for this, such as their withholding calculator[23] and simulation module.[24] Both of these resources serve as far more appropriate methods for tax planning than simply selecting the number of your dependents. Remember, the goal is to withhold enough money to pay your taxes but not so much that you get a substantial refund. I realize that some of you look at the April windfall as an annual "bonus," but in reality you could be making that money work for you throughout the year.

One more thing before we move away from the W-4. Unlike insurance choices, your W-4 can be changed at *any* time. I know that you're slammed with paperwork when you start a new job. This is why it's important to focus on the benefits and to make sure you're

---

[22] www.irs.gov

[23] https://www.irs.gov/Individuals/IRS-Withholding-Calculator

[24] https://apps.irs.gov/app/understandingTaxes/student/simulations.jsp

choosing the best options for health care and insurance. These types of benefits are usually annual or "change-of-life" options; that is, you can only make changes to them at certain times and under certain circumstances. On the other hand, you can modify your tax withholding amount at any point. I'm not telling you to switch it every month, but let's say you get a second job or have a baby—these would be great reasons to reevaluate your withholding amount. Just know that this document isn't set in stone for an entire year.

Tax Time—Keeping Good Records

So it's the end of January, and you've received your W-2 from your employer and other tax materials. Let's gather up all of your receipts and other paperwork. If you're like some clients I've worked with, this is the portion of tax time that really stresses you out. A friend once confessed to me that she just threw all of her receipts into a kitchen drawer and then took the drawer to her tax specialist! While this is not the ideal way to maintain documentation—or make friends with your tax person—I suppose it's a start.

I can't stress enough the importance of keeping complete and supportable documentation in order to reduce your income taxes. I encourage you to establish a paper or electronic file to store your essential tax documents throughout and after the end of the tax year—preferably NOT a kitchen drawer. This way, when all of your tax statements arrive in January, you can put or scan them into your file and presto—you're ready to talk taxes!

Being organized will take the stress out of tax time. It's essential that all of your materials are complete. You don't want to risk losing documents that can justify deductions. With today's vast array of recordkeeping and accounting software programs such as Quicken and QuickBooks, it's easy to download information from banks and mortgage companies, and to keep records so that all of your materials are in one place. In addition, these documents are required by law if you plan on itemizing deductions. Do yourself—and your tax person—a favor: keep good records! Trust me, it's not that hard to do, and in the end, you'll reap the benefits in reduced stress and in seeing how those deductions come in handy.

It Pays to Consult a Professional

Speaking of deductions, it's been my experience that if you're not using a 1040-EZ form—in other words, if you're itemizing deductions—then it's truly in your best interest to consult a tax professional. I'm not saying you have to hire a $500 per hour CPA, but I strongly encourage you to find a highly-qualified tax person to help you. I know, there's a myriad of tax software available, but trust me when I tell you this: it's worth the extra hundred bucks to hire a pro. All it takes is one tax season with a professional to convince you. A friend, "Allie," told me she owed the government nearly $4,000 the last time she used a tax software program to prepare her taxes. The following year, Allie hired a tax professional and received a refund of nearly $5,000. Her tax person informed her that she hadn't been taking all of her deductions. Want to guess if Allie ever did her taxes herself again?

Here's the deal: tax professionals know what deductions to look for and ways to save you money. Plus, they also know which types of expenses and amounts will most likely cause an IRS audit. If you're itemizing deductions, chances are you'll get the extra cost back, and then some, if you hire a pro. And the best part of this? The amount you pay for tax preparation is a tax deduction! No kidding. Uncle Sam will let you deduct this expense.

In addition to finding deductions, your tax person can advise you on ways to save money throughout the year. When you're meeting with your tax advisor, be sure to review your current W-4 amount to ensure you're not withholding too much or too little. A tax professional can offer guidance regarding the tax benefits of contributing the maximum amount to your employer-sponsored retirement plan. Plus, she can tell you if you qualify for either of the new tax-favored savings accounts, such as myRa[25] (for low income

---

[25] https://myra.gov

earners) and ABLE[26] (for disabled individuals). Use the time as an opportunity to evaluate the year ahead and see where you need to make adjustments to income and expenses.

If you've gone through a divorce during the tax year, it's even more important that you consult a tax professional. The tax code states that if you're unmarried on the last day of the year, you are considered unmarried for the *entire* year. This includes being legally separated from your spouse under a legally separated or divorce decree. You then have the option to file as single or head of household, the latter of which could save you taxes if you pay more than half the expenses of a qualifying dependent who lived with you for more than half a year.

As a result of the separation or divorce, your divorce attorney will discuss how tax-affected items are treated. These typically include how tax exemptions for dependents are claimed, how income is split, and how certain deductions such as mortgage interest, medical expenses, and prior tax payments are allocated. Most importantly, if there are tax refunds due, your attorney will address who's entitled to receive them.

Whether it's advising you on your filing status or protecting you from being liable for previous-year tax returns related to your partner's understated income, you need a tax professional to help guide you through your first post-divorce tax return.

Determining Your Filing Status

Married couples sometimes wonder if it would be in their best interest to file under the classification Married Filing Separately. Depending on your financial situation, there could definitely be some benefits to this option. One of the most advantageous aspects of this classification is that each spouse is only responsible for their own tax liability. This means if one spouse owes taxes, interest, and/or penalties, then the other spouse isn't responsible for the debt.

---

[26] National Disability Institute. "Real Economic Impact | ABLE Act." Real Economic Impact | ABLE Act. Accessed May 11, 2016. https://www.realeconomicimpact.org/public-policy/able-act

Plus, filing separately helps protect you in the event your spouse files fraudulent or inaccurate taxes. Of course, I suggest you consult with your tax professional before making the decision to file separately, but let's explore some of the pros and cons to this filing status.

If you and your partner both have large salaries, filing separately will prevent you from being bumped into an overall higher tax bracket if you combined incomes on a joint return. Another situation when filing separately works to your advantage is when one person has excessive medical expenses. Because certain deductions are limited to income, filing a joint return when the other person has a higher income may unknowingly cause those medical expenses to be only partially or not at all deductible.

Depending on your individual incomes, filing a joint return might adversely affect a student loan or subsidy approval. Also, certain deductions and credits that may be allowable on a joint return are sometimes limited or phased out on a Married Filing Separately return. Because tax code is quite complex, I suggest you consult with your tax advisor to determine which filing status is more advantageous to you in your given circumstances.

Help from Uncle Sam

I think Uncle Sam gets a bad rap. Want to know what a good friend he is? There are countless deductions he allows you to make in order to improve your quality of life. These deductions range from job hunting expenses to lifetime learning to paying for the babysitter if the sitter is watching your kids while you're working. Heck, you can even deduct the cost of having your taxes done by a professional! In addition to deductions, Uncle Sam offers pre-tax savings on retirement plans, health savings plans, insurance premiums, and many other payroll deduction expenses. And should you happen to have difficulty paying your back income taxes, the IRS has a program called the "Fresh Start Program" that enables you to pay your tax balance plus interest over seventy-two months, provided the amount owed is $50,000 or less. This program helps you avoid liens and levies on assets. And an added bonus is that it doesn't appear on your credit report.

Although the tax code may seem incredibly complex, Uncle Sam offers tools and guidance at IRS.gov to make things more straightforward. So, sure, we have to pay taxes, and if we've underpaid throughout the year we'll need to pony-up and pay our share by April 15th. If we plan and keep good records throughout the year though, this can be avoided. Tax time may not be *fun*, but it certainly doesn't have to be overwhelming either. With the right help—whether it's from the very useful guidance at the IRS website or assistance from a tax professional—you can finish your taxes and create a valuable financial snapshot to guide your decisions in the upcoming year.

Financial Questions to Ask About Taxes

1. Should I change the withholding amounts on my W-4 if too much or too little money is being taken from my paycheck?

2. Am I taking all my eligible deductions?

3. What planning can I do now in order to lower my taxes all year long?

4. Should I defer some income to next year in order to avoid being bumped into a higher tax bracket?

5. Am I putting the maximum amount of tax-free money into all of my retirement plans?

6. Do I qualify for either of the new tax-favored savings accounts, such as myRa (for low income earners) and ABLE (for disabled individuals)?

7. Should I decrease my income or increase my deductions to avoid getting into a higher tax bracket?

8. Should I file a Married Filing Separately or Married Filing Joint return?

9. What are my options if I've underpaid taxes and owe the IRS money?

Let's Hear from the Expert

Carolyn Kitty

Carolyn Kitty is a Chicago CPA and business consultant with over thirty years of individual and business tax experience.

My partner takes care of the taxes every year, so the only thing I have to do is sign them. Aren't I lucky?

No, you're NOT lucky! Never sign a tax return unless you understand what it contains. If your significant other handles all the finances, be sure to ask questions and get answers before signing off on ANY tax return. You might be surprised later when the expected refund doesn't arrive because of something your partner did . . . or didn't do! Keep in mind that when your signature is on the return, you're equally liable for what it contains.

I've read that there have been problems with identity theft and fraudulent tax returns. What can I do to protect myself?

You're absolutely right! You need to protect yourself against identity theft. The IRS paid out $5.8 billion in fraudulent refunds in 2014 alone. This is an ever-growing problem for the IRS and for taxpayers in terms of both time and money. Here are some ways that you can protect your identify:

- Read your bank and credit card statements every month and report any charge which appears suspicious.
- Review your social security statement to confirm your correct wage information. You can do this by signing up for an electronic account at www.SSA.gov.
- Shred any documents with personal and financial information, particularly those with your social security number.
- ID thieves send out emails and make phone calls purporting to be IRS representatives. The IRS will always contact taxpayers by snail mail, so if you suspect such a scam, report the call or the email to the IRS at 1-800-366-4484.

- Review each of your three credit reports at least once a year. Visit www.annualcreditreport.com to get your free reports.

I always dread tax day and having to do taxes. What are some positives about this time of the year?

Tax time is a good opportunity to review your year financially and to revisit estate planning documents, such as beneficiary designations, wills, and powers of attorney. It's also a good time to review your employee plan at work and ask questions, such as could you increase your retirement contribution for the coming year? Even another 1 percent will help make your future more secure. Are there other plans that your employer offers that you might opt into? Are you eligible to make a Roth IRA contribution? In other words, rather than look at tax time as a painful experience, think of it as the perfect moment to reflect on your financial health and review what changes you should make in order to start the next tax year on better footing.

Wrap-Up

Why You Need to Talk about Taxes

1. Don't ever Ever, EVER sign a tax return unless you've read and understood it. Your signature on a tax return makes you legally liable for its contents.

2. Before you ask your boss for a raise or taxable perks, know your current tax bracket and determine if the raise will knock you into a higher bracket.

3. If possible, defer income or increase deductible expenses in order to avoid moving into a higher tax bracket.

4. Divorce can complicate your taxes. If you're unmarried on the last day of the year, the IRS considers you unmarried for the entire year. Make sure your divorce attorney walks you through the details, such as how tax exemptions for dependents are claimed and how income is split.

5. There are advantages and disadvantages to Married Filing Separately. Consult a tax professional to determine which status best suits your situation and needs.

6. Don't give Uncle Sam a freebie loan by withholding too much money. Instead of getting an April refund windfall, put that money into an interest-bearing account or investment.

7. There are lots of great tax resources at www.irs.gov. Use them! They have everything from withholding calculators to tax simulators.

8. You can change the amount of money you want to withhold for taxes at any time during the calendar year. Unlike most employment benefits, you can always make adjustments to your tax withholding amount.

9. Get organized and keep records. Create either a paper or electronic file for receipts, mileage, and other deductions.

10. Take your taxes to a tax professional if you itemize deductions or have been through a divorce. These folks know taxes and ways to save you money. Plus, they can

advise you for the next year's tax season. You might spend a little more on a tax person than you would on a DIY tax software program, but it's worth the extra bucks. Plus, your tax preparation fee is a deductible expense.

11. Taxes aren't that difficult, and Uncle Sam isn't the boogey man. Stop being intimidated by them. Instead, think of tax time as an annual financial review. It's a great opportunity for you to look at and make changes to your income and expenses.

Let's Talk about Children

It's not what you do for your children, but what you have taught them to do for themselves, that will make them successful human beings.

Ann Landers

Chapter 6

Closing the Bank of Mom: Helping Your Adult Children Stand on Their Own Two Feet

Okay, girlfriends, if there was ever an aspect of my financial past that I'd like to do over, it's being a good financial role model for my children. I'll be the first to admit I've made mistakes when it comes to my kids and teaching them about money. Thankfully, they've all grown up to be responsible adults, but it's by sheer luck and newfound determination.

Becoming The Bank of Mom

Maybe it's because I was a single mom raising twin boys and a daughter on my own, but there was no way I was going to let my little angels live an impoverished life. When my first husband died from leukemia and left me almost penniless, I suddenly became Wonder Woman. You know that mom who lifts the car off of her baby? Well, that was me. I wasn't going to allow anyone or anything to make my babies feel like they had anything less than all the other kids. It wasn't their fault they didn't have a dad, so I worked my ass off to ensure I could make up for their loss.

I've never been more focused and profit-driven in my whole life than I was after my husband died. I worked harder, pushed open doors where I wasn't welcome, and did everything possible to guarantee my children could have everything they wanted or dreamed about. I have to confess that a lot of this came from my Jewish guilt. Hey, what can I say? I'm a Jewish mom—we feel guilty about most everything. As a result, I couldn't bear to see my kids not have things their friends had. And let me tell you, we lived in Highland Park, a seriously upscale Chicago suburb, so my kids had it all.

My children went to the best schools, the best overnight camps, and even got cars when they turned sixteen. Were they spoiled? Oh, yeah. But at the time, it was my intense guilt and overprotective nature that I blamed. I felt as if I was *protecting* them by giving them these things. In retrospect, I realize that what I did was provide my children with an unrealistic view of life and potentially set them up for financial difficulties when they got older.

The problem with trying to raise financially responsible children is that you want them to learn how to make smart financial decisions, but you also don't want to see them fail. Maybe women have an overprotective gene that makes it a challenge to knowingly allow our children to make financial mistakes. Whatever it is, I *had* it. Until one day . . .

Shelly's Story

What changed my perspective was when I met "Shelly," a new client in her late sixties. Initially, I was shocked to learn that Shelly hadn't retired, but I quickly understood why this wasn't feasible when I began to review her finances. Shelly couldn't retire because she was still supporting her two adult children. That's right, Shelly was making her kids' car payments, contributing to their mortgages, and even paying for her grandchildren's private school tuition. In other words, this woman was supporting not just herself, but also her children and *their* children. There was no way Shelly could retire if this continued.

After talking to Shelly about these additional expenses and the hardship they were causing her, I couldn't help but relate to Shelly's financial dilemma. She wanted to retire, but she also wanted to be able to help her kids out with their expenses. Shelly had worked hard her entire life to make sure her children had designer clothing, nice cars, and everything she had when she was their age. However, and this is huge—Shelly *earned* these things. They were never *given* to her. She began working part-time jobs when she was a freshman in high school and had saved up enough money to buy her first car before she entered her senior year. Although her parents paid for her college education, Shelly won numerous scholarships and maintained a part-time job the entire time she attended Northwestern University. She immediately secured a job after graduation and hasn't stopped working since.

Shelly wanted to retire, but she was afraid she couldn't afford to do it. I explained to her that she most definitely *could* afford to retire, but she would need to eliminate some of her expenses—all of them related to the vast amount of money she gave her children every month. Shelly thought long and hard about this, and eventually agreed that she really needed to retire. Although she was afraid of having to break the news to her children, I felt a real sense of relief as Shelly came to terms with this decision.

It turned out that over the last decade, Shelly had subsidized her two children's lifestyles to the tune of over a million dollars. And let me tell you, Shelly wasn't living like a millionaire. In fact, she owned a modest home, drove an older used car, and had a meager savings account. Thank goodness she had a healthy pension that she hadn't raided, or she probably couldn't have afforded to *ever* retire.

I went home that night and couldn't get Shelly and her situation out of my head. I totally understood where she was coming from. And let's be honest, I could see myself being in her shoes if I continued to subsidize so many of my kids' activities and accounts. The thought of this scared me and got me thinking about the impact of Shelly's generosity. Not only was she preventing herself from having a relaxing retirement, but she was also enabling her children to overspend and creating a dependence on her income that would one day eventually end. Although Shelly thought she was doing something kind and loving for her kids, in reality, she was doing them a disservice. Sometimes what we think helps our children actually does the opposite.

Shelly called me a few days after our initial meeting and sounded quite distraught. The announcement that she would have to eliminate funding her children's extra expenses was not well-received. This came as no surprise. However, I wasn't expecting Shelly's next piece of news. She informed me that she would continue working for another year or two until her kids could "get back on their feet." In other words, she was going to postpone retirement for another year or two. My heart sank when Shelly told me this because I knew that she desperately needed a break. Just as I had when my children were younger, Shelly allowed her motherly instincts to overpower her common sense. I went home that night even more determined *not* to walk in Shelly's footsteps.

And let me tell you, Shelly isn't alone. According to a 2015 survey by American Consumer Credit Counseling, over half of the respondents say they provide financial support to at least one adult child. [27] This is a very concerning trend because the money these parents use to support their children should actually be going toward their retirement planning. As it is, most Baby Boomers have a huge retirement shortfall. According to a 2015 BlackRock report,[28] the average Boomer has accumulated a meager $136,200 in retirement savings, which is equivalent to an estimated $760.75 monthly paycheck. I talk more about retirement planning later in the book, but you don't have to be an Einstein to realize we need to stop supporting our adult children and begin putting that money away for retirement.

It's Never Too Early to Start Talking about Money with Your Children

Although I never included my own kids in financial talks, I'm now a firm believer in exposing children to money at an early age. I feel it's important to have open financial conversations as a whole

---

[27] "Providing Financial Support for Adult Children – ConsumerCredit.com." ConsumerCredit.com. Accessed May 13, 2016.
http://www.consumercredit.com/about-us/press-releases/2015-press-releases/fail ure-to-launch-syndrome-can-hurt-household-budgets.aspx
[28] "Americans focus on the right goals, but money attitudes, behaviors get in the way of financial success." BlackRock 2015 Annual Global Investor Pulse Survey: Accessed May 13, 2016.
http://www.blackrock.com/corporate/en-us/literature/press-release/gip-press-rele ase-2015.pdf

family instead of just parents behind closed doors.

Sadly, budgeting money is a skill many lack—young and old. However, there are many online tools for setting up a budget. One of my personal favorites is Every Dollar, a free resource from money guru, Dave Ramsey.[29] It takes dedication to get the most out of a budgeting tool such as Every Dollar, but when used daily, it can help the user stay within a set budget and save money.

Include your children in chats about the household budget so they gain an understanding of how much money has been budgeted for specific items such as groceries, dining out, and entertainment. Furthermore, explain why you have a budget and how you created it. Allowing your children to play an active role in the household budget not only shows them how to build and follow their own budget, but it offers a myriad of teaching opportunities about money. This is an ideal time to discuss the pros and cons of credit cards, what role your debt-to-income ratio plays when trying to get credit, and the importance of setting up an emergency cash fund. Becoming a good financial role model for your children when they're young will help prevent financial disasters when they're older.

It's never too early for your children to set a personal budget. Whether their sole income is from an allowance, a part-time job, or mowing lawns, *now* is the time to begin developing good financial habits that include saving money and sticking to a budget. While creating the budget, make sure you instill the value of saving. Even if your child is earning minimum wage at a nearby fast-food restaurant, teach him to pay himself first by socking away a percentage of each paycheck into savings. It may seem like an inconsequential amount of money, but it will cultivate a pattern of positive money habits and impart the importance of saving money.

Jenny's Story

"Jenny" and her husband wanted to be alive to see their kids enjoy some of their inheritance, so they gave their two children and

---

[29] "EveryDollar - Dave Ramsey Budget Tool - Daveramsey.com." Accessed May 13, 2016. https://www.daveramsey.com/everydollar

six grandchildren a one-time gift of $15,000 each. Jenny had grown up in an affluent household, but after marrying at a young age, she became quite frugal because her husband was still in school and money was extremely tight. Even though Jenny's husband later became partner in a prominent law firm, Jenny still maintained a strict hand on the family's finances and was very careful with money . . . except when it came to her children, and especially her daughter, "Melissa."

Jenny allowed her daughter to splurge on trendy clothes and new sports cars, and when Melissa got married, Jenny had no qualms upping the budget so her daughter could have the wedding of her dreams. Jenny was also extremely generous with her son, "Bryan," but instead of providing funds for clothing and cars, she and her husband often gave their son cash to put into a savings account.

Jenny came to see me nearly a year after presenting her family with the generous gifts. When I asked if the kids had been surprised, she smiled and said that she and her husband loved watching them have fun trying to decide what to do with their windfall. She told me that this was the best part of giving them the money.

Melissa and her three twenty-something daughters spent the bulk of their funds on a trip to Hawaii, clothing, jewelry, handbags, and shoes. In other words: they went on one heckuva shopping spree! When Jenny came to see me, none of them had anything left from the $15,000 they had received.

Bryan and his three children, on the other hand, not only still had the money, but they had all invested their gifts and were now sitting on nest eggs that had almost doubled in value. This was the first venture into investing for Bryan's college-aged kids, and after watching the money their grandmother had given them grow in value in such a short period of time, they were now avid investors.

Jenny wasn't surprised that her daughter and granddaughters had spent all of their money on clothes and such, and in no way did she regret giving them the money. However, it opened her eyes to the lessons about money she had given her children as they were growing up. Jenny and her husband never encouraged their daughter to save her money. Instead, Jenny eagerly cheered Melissa on as they browsed the racks at Nordstrom and Saks Fifth Avenue. In retrospect, Jenny wished she and her husband had instilled the same values and views of money in their daughter that they had given their son.

Let's Talk About Money with our Children

No matter how old or young your children are, talking about money with your kids should be just like talking about money with your partner or spouse. You need to be open and honest about your current financial situation.

However, rather than telling your kids that you "can't afford" something, use language that's more proactive, such as, "I've decided to spend my money this way." I'll never forget when one of my sons told me he wanted to buy several items but only had enough money for one. After asking me to "help him out," I declined and told him that adults encounter this dilemma nearly every day— "Should I spend my money on this . . . or that?"

I told him to be like an adult and *choose*!

If your child asks to return home after having tried living on their own, the first place to start is by letting them know your expectations for the arrangement. For example, when your recent college graduate wants to move back home until she finds a job, make sure you've created an agreement for the transition. This includes everything from how long she can stay to what she'll pay for while living with you. Also, clearly spell out what household duties you expect her to do. I know this might sound harsh, but trust me, I've seen way too many family feuds from move-back-home scenarios without these precautions in place.

Turn money requests into loans. If your child needs $5,000 to pay off credit card debt, don't just give it to him—loan him the money. Draft a loan agreement with set terms, an interest rate comparable to what banks are charging, and a repayment schedule with penalties for late payments. Have your child sign a legal contract making him bound to the terms. All requests for "help" should be treated as business transactions with specific plans for repayment. The financial help you give your children might not be large, but over time it can certainly add up.

Love Is Not About Money

I know I mentioned this in an earlier chapter, but it bears repeating: money is not love, and love is not money. It's a difficult concept to grasp, but it's vital you come to terms with it. I know too well the consequences of believing money and love are the same animal. I've been there, done that, and bought the postcard! Want to know what love is when dealing with your kids? It's teaching them to be independent and to make smart financial decisions, and it's showing them how to survive and thrive on their own. As the old saying goes, teach your kids to fish—to be financially savvy—so they can have independence and freedom forever. Now, *that* is love.

It's time for The Bank of Mom to shut its doors for good. If your kids are accustomed to the bank being open 24/7, this new "tough love" approach will most likely be met with some resistance. But stay strong. You want your adult children to become financially independent so they can stand on their own two feet. There will come a time when you won't be around to bail them out of their financial messes.

We all want to help our children, but we must remember to focus on *our* needs as well. I'm not saying the occasional request for support should be met with disapproval, but if it becomes a habit, keep in mind that the money you're doling out to your kids *should* be put toward your retirement plan. Your children have a lifetime of employment ahead of them, while you will eventually need to retire. Don't risk not having enough money to do so by spending your retirement funds supporting your adult children. If you *do*, there's a good chance that your kids will have to support *you*!

Financial Questions to Ask so Your Adult Children Can Stand on Their Own Two Feet

Parents

1. Have I included my children in financial discussions?

2. Do I allow my children to participate in the budgeting process?

3. How long have I been financially supporting my adult child? How much longer can I continue to provide this support?

4. What are the underlying reasons for providing support? Is it a feeling of guilt or overprotectiveness that keeps me offering financial assistance to my child?

5. Is the money I'm giving my adult child preventing me from retiring?

6. Am I willing to show "tough love" by forcing my adult children to stand on their own two feet?

Children

7. Have you created a realistic budget? Are you sticking to it?

8. Do you "pay yourself" first after receiving each paycheck?

9. Are you asking too much from your parents? Are you forcing your parents to make financial sacrifices?

Wrap-Up

Why You Need to Close the Doors to
the Bank of Mom

1. Supporting your adult children can delay retirement. While you might be able to pay your bills and those of your adult children while you're working, chances are your plan for retirement didn't include these extra expenses. As a result, you won't be able to retire when you want to.

2. Include and involve your children in the budgeting process. Be a good financial role model for your children now so that they become financially savvy adults.

3. Money is not love, and love is not money. Instead of giving your children money, teach them the tools to become financially independent.

4. Assist your child in setting up a realistic budget that he can stick to. This includes eliminating excessive spending and getting the best deals for services and credit cards.

5. Encourage your child to begin saving money from every paycheck. The money he puts away initially might be small, but it will help him develop the habit of saving.

6. If your child needs to move back home, have her sign an agreement clearly outlining your expectations regarding financial contributions, length of stay, house rules, and household responsibilities.

7. Consider any money your child requests as a loan. Draw up a loan agreement with an interest rate comparable to what banks charge, and a repayment schedule with penalties for late fees. This goes even for small amounts of money.

8. Every dollar that you give your adult child should actually go toward your retirement planning. Don't risk having too little money for retirement. Your children have a lifetime of employment ahead of them, but you don't. There are no scholarships for retirement.

Chapter 7

Forever in Debt: The Harsh Reality of Student Loans

Since the inception of federal student loans under the National Defense of Education Act of 1958,[30] students without the financial means have had the opportunity to borrow money in order to go to college. The Federal Family Loan Program has undergone many changes since the first student loan was administered, and it now offers a federally-guaranteed loan provided by banks and non-profit lenders.

In 2014, forty million Americans had at least one outstanding student loan.[31] Although the exact amount owed to student loan lenders isn't known, it's estimated to be between $1.4 to $1.32 trillion,[32] with the individual borrower having an average balance of at least $35,000.[33] This amount increases dramatically depending on school costs and if the student continues on to graduate school. If these figures haven't scared you enough, keep in mind that the amount of student loan debt has been consistently rising *every* year.

---

[30] "Atlas." Atlas. July 7, 2015. Accessed May 13, 2016.
http://atlas.newamerica.org/federal-student-loan-programs-history
[31] Ellis, Blake. "40 Million Americans Now Have Student Loan Debt."
CNNMoney. September 10, 2014. Accessed May 13, 2016.
http://money.cnn.com/2014/09/10/pf/college/student-loans/
[32] Nasiripour, Shahien. "The Federal Government Has No Idea How Much Americans Owe On Student Loans." The Huffington Post. March 5, 2015. Accessed May 13, 2016.
http://www.huffingtonpost.com/2015/03/05/government-student-loans_n_6808796.html
[33] Sparshott, Jeffrey. "Congratulations, Class of 2015. You're the Most Indebted Ever (For Now)." WSJ. May 8, 2015. Accessed May 13, 2016.
http://blogs.wsj.com/economics/2015/05/08/congratulations-class-of-2015-youre-the-most-indebted-ever-for-now/

If parents haven't been contributing to a 529 plan, a tax-free state educational savings plan, they sometimes offer to take out student loans for their kids. Whether parents opt for a Parent PLUS or private student loan, or worse, use equity from their home to pay for their child's education, the bottom line is this: the loan is theirs and theirs alone. I'll address this type of student loan later, along with the reasons for why this isn't a wise option.

Welcome to a Lifetime of Loan Repayment

In theory, student loans are a godsend for those who can't afford a college education without them. I totally understand and see the need for federal student loans. However, the reality is that a student loan can be a hefty debt the student carries for a decade or two. Students often accept these loans without realizing the impact of such a substantial obligation. I'm not just talking about the enormous monthly loan payments that your child will be paying for the next twenty years. I'm also referring to the influence it will have on marriage, employment, the ability to purchase a home, and more. All of these things can be affected by your child's student loan debt.

The application process is painless compared to the repayment. It's shocking just how easy it is to apply and get approved for a federal student loan. An applicant just needs to submit a Free Application for Federal Student Aid (FAFSA) on-time, wait until they receive an offer, accept it, and BAM!—they now have a loan for thousands of dollars. Because federal student loans are based on need rather than credit history, even students or families who have terrible credit can receive them.

Depending on the type of loan, repayment begins within six months after graduation. There's no wasting time! And let me tell you, lenders will let you know the second you graduate that the clock has started. In addition to your child receiving graduation cards and gifts, he'll also get a large envelope from the student loan lenders outlining the loans and a repayment schedule. It's all a little intimidating and a whole lot scary.

Many students opt to consolidate their loans so that they're making only one payment per month. However, what they often don't realize is that in doing this, they extend the length of their loan. For example, the standard repayment schedule is often calculated so the debt is paid off in ten years, as opposed to up to thirty years for a consolidated loan.

Lenders usually offer a variety of repayment plans because few students are able to begin making large loan payments so soon after graduation. Your child must qualify for some options, such as the Income-Based Repayment and Income-Based Contingent plans. Some also offer loan forgiveness after a specific period of repayment. For example, the Pay-as-You-Earn Repayment Plan forgives the remaining balance after you've made payments consistently for twenty years.

Some students also defer or forbear their student loan payments. Both of these options require documentation and approval depending on the type of deferment or forbearance. While this might sound like an excellent option for those who are either unemployed or underemployed, keep in mind that interest accrues daily on most loans. In other words, if you put your loan in forbearance for a year, you're not only going to be responsible for the original amount of the loan, but also for the interest the loan has accrued during the time it was in forbearance. In the end, you're going to owe considerably more money than when you started.

Although there are a few forgiveness programs for student loans, the majority of borrowers have only one way to erase the debt: pay it off. Even if you hit rock bottom and have to file for bankruptcy, you're still required to repay your student loans.

Amy's Story

Many students willingly accept the maximum amount offered by a student loan lender without considering the ramifications of this action. A client, "Amy," recently came to see me because her relationship with "Mike" had gotten serious, and she was contemplating marriage.

Amy and Mike had worked together for several years, but it

wasn't until a year before Amy came to see me that they became a couple. Taking my advice, Amy had had the money conversation with him. During their chat, Mike informed Amy that he owed nearly $150,000 in student loans. Although Mike earned a sizable income, his student loan payments ate a chunk of his paycheck.

Amy also had student debt, but it was only a third of Mike's. Their combined student loan amounts concerned Amy greatly. She had already experienced the impact of having this large debt on her credit rating when she applied for the mortgage on her small condominium.

Breaking down in tears, Amy told me that she wasn't sure if she should marry Mike because they would have combined student loan debt of nearly $200,000. As well as worrying about the amount of money they would be spending each month to repay their loans, Amy was also afraid that they wouldn't qualify for a home loan due to the excessive amount of their student loans. She knew that if she married Mike and his $150,000 student loan, her life was going to be financially difficult.

I don't mean to sound unromantic, but I think Amy was incredibly smart to consider this aspect of her relationship. She was absolutely right in thinking that such a large debt would impact their future. While most creditors look at student loan debt as "good" debt, it's debt nonetheless. And $200,000 is no laughing matter. It's essentially the same as paying for a second home.

I praised Amy for her foresight and explained that it was truly a decision she would have to make herself. That said, I also told her that she and Mike could make themselves desirable to lenders if they worked on their debt-to-income ratio. This might involve extending their current loan repayment plans, though. If Mike had been making payments based on the standard plan, he would now have lower payments, but for a longer period of time. Although this might not be ideal for Mike and Amy's future, at least it would help them when applying for a mortgage or auto loan.

Student Loan Debt—It's Not Just Our Children's Problem

The problem of student loan debt isn't restricted to our kids. Many adults are now returning to school for advanced degrees, only to find themselves burdened with student loans.

When I gasped at the amount my new client, "Cynthia," owed in student loans, she shook her head in disgrace. She confessed that she had never paid too much attention to the amount when she was in school. Because she worked full-time as a high school English teacher, Cynthia attended school part-time and took six years to complete her Master's degree. She applied for student loans every year and accepted the maximum amount offered. Some years she received as much as $24,000 for the school year. When she finished her degree, she found herself owing over $140,000 to various lenders.

Cynthia told me that she honestly hadn't realized exactly how much she'd borrowed while she was in school. She recalled receiving emails and packages from various lenders after she graduated and admitted that she had no idea who the lenders were until they contacted her.

Cynthia had initially returned to school because she would receive a pay increase for having a Master's degree. But she no longer requires her expensive education degree because she recently quit teaching.

Sadly, Cynthia isn't alone. Many adults return to school only to find themselves with an unnecessary advanced degree and large student loan debt. Having just celebrated her fifty-second birthday, Cynthia now realizes that her decision to take on such financial responsibility at this point in her life will jeopardize her ability to ever retire. She jokingly told me that she will probably work forever and will most likely die without having paid off her student loans.

In addition to owing on their own student loan, parents are often torn as to whether or not they should take out a federal or private loan for their child's education. Let's say Tommy gets accepted to his dreamed-about out-of-state college to the tune of $60,000 per semester. He's eligible for $13,000 in federal financial aid, but it's up to you to come up with the remaining $47,000. What's a loving parent to do? Federal Direct PLUS loans to the rescue. Although PLUS loans require a credit check, the guidelines for lending are minimal—you just can't have any adverse credit activity on your credit report—so they're fairly easy to obtain. These PLUS loans allow parents to borrow as much as necessary to send their kid to school, at a cost.

A *very high* cost!

At the time of this publication, Parent PLUS loans can be consolidated, but most can't be repaid under an income-based repayment plan. The most important detail about these loans, though, is that the loans are in the parents' names—*forever*. You can't change the loan to your child's name once he graduates. No, the parent will *always* be responsible for repayment. Not only does this impact the parents' income-to-debt ratio and FICO score, but all lower payment and deferment options are based on the parents' income instead of the entry-level student's salary. And kiss those opportunities for loan forgiveness away. Parent PLUS loans aren't eligible for these perks either.

Maybe you're contemplating co-signing for either a Parent PLUS or private bank loan for your child. Again, I can't caution you enough to *not* do this. I'll remind you that co-signers are just as responsible for the debt as the original applicant. Furthermore, this debt will also appear on your credit report.

Tackling this kind of debt when you're approaching retirement is not wise for the majority of parents. I understand that you want to give your kids the best education possible, but you don't want to risk not being able to retire.

Let's Talk about the Five Golden Rules of Student Loans

Let's say you've made sure there are no employer tuition incentive programs that you can apply to and you're not eligible for scholarships based on your ethnicity, gender, religion, or parent's employer. Sometimes there are no other alternatives to obtaining a student loan. However, there are five golden rules you need to know before you take out a student loan.

Rule number one is to *only* accept the amount absolutely necessary for tuition and fees *after you've exhausted all other avenues of funding*. After receiving their student loan awards letter, most students eagerly accept the large sums of cash offered to them by lenders. Rarely do they take only what they need to pay for college, but instead, they opt for the maximum amount and use it for living expenses . . . or pizza and beer. At the time, it feels like free money.

Well, it's not free, and some of those loans are accruing interest the minute your child picks up the check. Make sure your child understands that he'll start making payments on that "free money" six months after he graduates. Borrow today and pay forever.

The next rule is to keep a record of all student loans. You might be surprised by how many students graduate without a clue as to how much they owe and from whom they borrowed the money. Your child needs to keep a detailed account of the funds received and the repayment terms. Also, make notes of loans that are currently accruing interest, and if at all possible, pay this amount monthly.

Rule number three is to keep working. Once they're in school, students often use classwork and lack of time as an excuse to quit their part-time jobs. This is a big no-no. Sure, school can keep your kid busy, but having a part-time job not only provides your child with an income, it also creates time management skills and hopefully develops a pattern of saving. When your child has to work to help pay for his education, I guarantee he'll put more effort into his studies.

A friend, "Marcy," recently graduated with a Master's degree. Marcy finished her degree with a 4.0 GPA and told me that she wished she had worked that hard during her undergraduate years. She said that her parents paid for her Bachelor's degree, but having to shell out the money for graduate school herself, she found she never cut class and constantly devoted herself to her studies. She had a professor one semester who was always cancelling classes because he was traveling. Marcy joked that she thought the professor owed the students a refund. There's something about having to contribute to the cost of your education that makes you appreciate it a little more.

The fourth rule before your child takes out a student loan pertains to her choice of college. All too often, students want to attend a school because of a successful football team or geography. But here's the thing—you can get a perfectly fine undergraduate degree at your local state university for a fraction of the cost of an out-of-state school. Tuition usually triples for out-of-state colleges. Unless your child is studying some specific subject or needs to work with a particular professor, there is absolutely no need to go into extreme debt for the next twenty years in order to obtain a Bachelor's degree.

Finally, I encourage your child to weigh the profitability of his degree against the amount of his student loan. I'm not saying, for example, that your child shouldn't get an education degree because teachers are poorly paid. But he needs to look at his income potential post-graduation to get a sense of what kind of burden he may have paying back loans. At the very least, it may inspire him to accept the smallest loan he needs rather than grabbing the maximum he's offered. Trust me, there are loads of humanities graduates desperate for a job. The problem is they're not sure what they're qualified to do. Before your child invests four years and at least $35,000 in a college education, he needs to know how he's going to earn an income after he graduates. While being a theatre major might be fun, you have to think about how you can market yourself with that degree. Don't let your child make the mistake of choosing a major he can't support.

Financial Questions to Ask Before Accepting a Student Loan

Parents

1. Have I completed my child's FAFSA correctly?
2. If I take out a student loan for my child, can I transfer it to his name after he graduates?
3. Will my child's student loan (in my name) impact my FICO score?
4. Can my child's student loan (in my name) be consolidated or eligible for an income-based repayment plan?
5. Can my child's student loan (in my name) be discharged or forgiven?

Students

6. Am I eligible for any employer tuition incentive programs?
7. Am I eligible for any scholarships based on my ethnicity, gender, religion, or parents' employers?
8. Can my student loan be discharged, forgiven, or cancelled? If so, when and how?
9. When do I have to begin loan repayment?
10. Can I modify my loan payment? Can it be less or more?
11. What loans accrue interest while I'm in school?
12. What happens if I don't make my student loan payment?
13. Will the student loan impact my FICO score?

Let's Hear from the Expert

Lora Georgieva

Lora Georgieva is a Certified College Planner and the founder of Destination College. Her mission is to help families plan and pay for college without going broke.

What's the number one college planning mistake?

Going into the college application process completely blind and too late. If your child is already high school age, the best time to start planning is the beginning of the junior year. Many families wait until the beginning of the senior year in high school to start researching their options. By this time, some of their options are gone or they have to rush to complete the process. Also, it's important your child has excellent academic achievements from freshman through senior year. College planning actually begins the minute your child begins high school.

What is the best time to start financial planning for college?

The answer is now! The longer you wait to start saving, the less money you will accumulate for college.

How do I increase my chances of getting a scholarship?

Do research on the sponsor of the scholarship and learn about the organization's mission. For example, if the scholarship committee supports world peace, talking about your World War II grandfather veteran might not be a good idea. Instead, you would want to mention why you are passionate about world peace and how you are contributing to it.

What do I need to do to apply for financial aid?

The first thing you have to do is complete the Free Application for Federal Student Aid (FAFSA) application on time. Financial aid is distributed on a first-come, first-served basis, so the longer you wait, the less chance you have of getting maximum financial assistance. FAFSA will qualify you for federal, state, and institutional grants and loans. With some schools, that amount can be as much as $60,000 per year if you file early enough.

Also be sure to submit the Financial Aid PROFILE® form located on the College Board website.[34] This form is required by approximately three hundred private colleges nationwide when applying for any university grants. If you don't submit it on time, you will be disqualified from receiving these funds.

What if I am unemployed but my tax return shows high income?

You can file a special circumstances appeal if you are experiencing hardship through reduction of income, high medical expenses or disability, or if you have an inflated income on your tax return due to something like an inheritance or a one-time bonus. File an appeal with the financial aid office and notify them of your circumstances.

How many times should I take the ACT exam?

I suggest you take the test at least three times. Just a single point difference can result in better admission chances or increased scholarships.

Should I apply early to universities?

Absolutely YES! You have the best chance of receiving scholarships when you apply early. Some universities offer full tuition, and those scholarships are due very early in the process. You typically need to apply by November 1st.

Do I need to go on college visits?

Yes. Visiting the admission's office will increase your chances of getting into the university because admissions officers keep track of the students who visit the university prior to submitting applications. Your college visit can make the difference between an acceptance letter or a rejection.

---

[34] "CSS / Financial Aid PROFILE®." Apply for College Financial Aid – CSS/Financial Aid PROFILE – The College Board. Accessed May 13, 2016. https://student.collegeboard.org/css-financial-aid-profile

Wrap-Up

Why You Need to Talk to Your Children about Student Loan Debt

1. Student loans are a godsend for those who truly need them, but bear in mind that the borrower will be paying them back for the next ten to twenty years.

2. Student loans are not dischargeable in bankruptcy. The only way to erase student loan debt is to either qualify for forgiveness or repay the loan.

3. Student loans can impact more than your bank account. Excessive student loan debt can affect your relationships, your credit score, and your ability to get a mortgage.

4. Returning students who take out student loans must understand that these loans can jeopardize their retirement.

5. Parents who take out student loans for their children or who co-sign on these loans are responsible for repayment. Loans that are in the parents' names can't be changed; the loan is in the parents' names forever.

6. The five golden rules of accepting a student loan are:

    ➢ Only accept the loan amount to cover tuition. Don't accept the maximum amount offered.

    ➢ Keep a record of all loans, along with a note of what loans are currently accruing interest. If possible, pay interest on these loans while still in school.

    ➢ Keep working. Students who have to contribute to the cost of their education tend to work harder and get better grades.

    ➢ Stick to home. Don't choose an out-of-state school when local state schools offer a quality education.

    ➢ Weigh the profitability of your degree. Choose a marketable major that can support repayment of your student loan.

Let's Talk about Parents

Love your parents. We are so busy growing up, we often forget they are busy growing old.

Unknown

Chapter 8

You're NOT Being Greedy: It's Time to Lose the Stigma of Talking about Your Parents' Estate

I realize that discussing estate planning with your parents isn't easy, but it's an incredibly important conversation to have in order to ensure that your parents' end-of-life wishes are followed. Over 50 percent of American adults don't have a will or other form of estate planning.[35] That percentage increases dramatically among minority populations. When you die without a will, there's no guarantee as to who will inherit your property and assets. Furthermore, there will be increased tax consequences and the need to send the estate to probate.

You're Not Being Greedy . . . You're Being Smart

I've worked with many clients who told me they feared having the discussion about their parents' estate because they didn't want to come across as being greedy. But there's nothing greedy about urging your parents to plan—it's smart. It's important that your parents bequeath their assets as they desire. And furthermore, children need to accept their parents' wishes.

Justine's Story

A client, "Justine," was a doting daughter to her widowed father,

---

[35] Kennedy, A. L. "Statistics on Last Wills & Testaments." LegalZoom: Legal Info. Accessed May 13, 2016.
http://info.legalzoom.com/statistics-last-wills-testaments-3947.html

"Geoffrey." Justine and her family lived close to her dad and saw him daily. Her two brothers lived across the country and rarely came home to visit. They were both businessmen with families. They led hectic lives and were delighted that Justine was close enough to help care for their aging father.

Although Geoffrey had a heart condition, he tried to stay active and was a regular at his grandchildren's basketball and baseball games. He treasured the time he had with Justine and her family and recognized the extra effort his daughter made to ensure he was always a part of the family's events and Sunday meals.

One night after dinner, Geoffrey told Justine that in addition to a third of his assets, he wanted to leave his house to her. Justine was uncomfortable with this news. She worried her brothers might be upset because she would end up with a greater portion of their parents' estate. Geoffrey said that he didn't care about this because it was his house, and he wanted to leave it to his devoted daughter. He argued that if she hadn't been around to help him, he would probably be in a retirement community or nursing home. He saw the house as his way of thanking her for making his last years of life so enjoyable.

Justine mulled around this offer for quite a while. She was touched that her father wanted to leave his house to her, but she was also concerned that accepting it would create animosity between her and her siblings. She finally told her dad that she would like him to include the house in the entire estate and not leave it all to her. Geoffrey was taken aback by Justine's decision but agreed to do as she wished.

Geoffrey suffered a fatal heart attack later that year. Per Justine's wishes, he had left his will as it had originally been written, with the house equally divided between his three children. It wasn't until Justine's husband lost his job the following year and the family endured a very difficult time financially that Justine began to wish she had taken her father up on his offer. They could have used the extra funds during this rough time.

When Justine lamented about declining her father's offer, I

reminded her that she had been her father's caregiver, and I was sure he felt it was fair to leave the house to her. I asked Justine how she would have felt if she had made such an offer to her daughter and received the same response. It was then that Justine realized what a painful mistake she had made. Yes, she could have used the money from the sale of the house, but most importantly, she had prevented her father from giving her a gift that he truly wanted to give. Justine cried at this revelation and told me that she declined because she didn't want her dad or her brothers to think she was greedy. I assured her that given the circumstances, this most likely wouldn't have been the case.

When parents tell you they want to leave a specific asset to you in their will, I encourage you to graciously accept the offer and not argue. Accepting such a proposal is not a sign of greediness. In Justine's case, it was a way of allowing her dad to thank her for the kindness, care, and love she had shown him while he was alive. I'm confident that if Justine had contacted her brothers and informed them of their father's offer, her siblings would have understood and been pleased for her.

Death is Inevitable . . . Plan Ahead

Another common mistake I see is when parents want to discuss estate plans with their children, but the conversation is brushed aside with the excuse that death is too sad to talk about. Well, as far as I know, we're all eventually going to die. And yes, nobody wants a loved one to pass away, but here's the thing about estate planning: when an estate is planned, your parents can take their last breath knowing that their affairs are in order and their assets are well-protected. I'd never fly to Europe without leaving my travel plans and instructions for my family in case of an emergency. Estate planning is basically the same thing. It's a way to protect your loved ones when you're gone.

Katie's Story

A friend, "Katie," recently lost her mother, "Jane," to cancer.

Katie was heartbroken by the loss, but thanks to her mother's astute estate planning, the legal side of her mother's death was quite simple. Jane made it a point to educate her daughter about her will and living will. There was no question what should be done when Jane was in her final days. Katie had been appointed her mother's power of attorney and estate trustee. She had Jane's health care directive on hand for the Hospice medical team, and after her mother's death, she had easy access to all of Jane's legal documents.

Because Jane was so forthright with her estate planning, Katie never felt uncomfortable discussing her mother's end-of-life wishes. Jane approached the topic of estate planning with a practical, no-nonsense attitude. She stressed that through her planning she was protecting her assets by ensuring she left them to those whom she loved.

Whether it's you or your parents who open the conversation about estate planning, know that there is nothing morbid about the topic. When parents ask to discuss their estate with you, it's important to listen carefully and ask questions. At some point, you'll need to know as much as possible about these plans.

There's More to Estate Planning Than Writing a Will

Most people automatically assume that creating a will is all that's necessary when planning an estate. However, there's so much more to it than this. Before your parents meet with an estate attorney, it's advisable to discuss the elements of estate planning.

A will is a legal document that designates how assets will be distributed upon death and who will act as representative during probate. Estates without this document will go to probate where a judge has full control over deciding how assets are divided and who is to act for the estate. Not having a will creates a mess for your grieving loved ones, so make sure your parents have a will in place.

In addition to a will, your parents might want to consider setting up a living trust. A living trust allows you to place your assets in a trust so that they're protected while you're alive and can then be distributed after death. A trustee is named when creating a living trust. The trustee oversees the trust while the grantor is alive, as well as after his death. Often, the grantor and the trustee are one and the same until age or health issues come into play.

There are quite a few advantages to a living trust. For one, living trusts help minimize inheritance taxes. Another benefit includes avoiding probate; this in turn helps keep your financial affairs private. When an estate is sent to probate, it becomes a matter of public record. Although some people might not care if their finances are made public, many prefer to keep that information private.

Living trusts are usually revocable, and because they're living documents, they can be changed when needed. However, parents might wish to create an irrevocable trust in order to ensure a beneficiary receives their designated portion. Because irrevocable trusts usually can't be changed or terminated by anyone without the permission of the beneficiary, assets are protected in the event of remarriage after death of the grantor. Since this type of trust can't be changed, great care should be used in drafting an irrevocable trust.

Other aspects of estate planning include health care directives and designation of Power of Attorney (POA). A health care directive is exactly as its name implies: it provides guidance on health care decisions. There are two types of POA—health care and financial. The health care POA acts as a medical advocate and ensures all health care directives are observed. The financial POA oversees financial matters when a loved one is unable to handle their financial affairs. Both of these POAs should be trusted individuals (and can be the same individual) who will act in your parents' best interest. I have known quite a few clients and friends who made the mistake of choosing POAs who took advantage of their role, so have your parents choose wisely.

While planning their estate, your parents will identify the beneficiaries of their assets. This should include any pets they might own. Many animals are sent to shelters after the loss of their owners, so make sure your parents have made arrangements for the care of their beloved pets. In addition, they will name the executor/trustee they want to be in charge of making sure that their wishes are honored. Naming the executor/trustee is an important part of the planning process.

Additional pieces of estate planning can include funeral arrangements, charitable giving designations, and a business plan of succession. Depending on your parents' estate, there might be more items to consider, but fear not: a good estate attorney will be thorough and will make the process painless.

Let's Talk about Estate Planning

The best way to open the conversation about estate planning with your parents is to have done your own estate planning first. Setting an example for your parents by having seen an estate attorney to write your own plan easily opens the door to this potentially touchy topic. You can say, "I just did estate planning with an attorney. I feel so much more secure and relieved knowing that this has been done. Have you seen an estate planning attorney?" In addition to scoring points for being extremely responsible, this action gives you an opportunity to discuss your own plan with your parents.

Another way of starting the discussion is to mention you've spoken to your financial professional (advisor, coach, attorney, CPA) about a checklist of items that are important for the family's financial security and safety. From there, you can review the checklist with your parents. While there is a chance your parents might not want to talk about estate planning, you should be able to discover if there's a plan in place.

You can also broach this topic with your parents by letting them know that you want to ensure their end-of-life wishes are carried out. Estate planning is more than simply designating who gets what assets. It also includes medical and health care desires. Many people have specific end-of-life wishes, such as a Do Not Resuscitate (DNR) order. It's important that children are aware of these requests before they're unable to consult the parent about them. There is nothing worse than children trying to decide what to do when a parent is on life support. A living will provides direction in medical events and eliminates the need for such major decisions.

Talking to your parents about estate planning should be relatively painless. Yes, it's a topic that many of us would rather ignore, but death happens whether we want it to or not. Instead of focusing on the sadness of the subject, look at it from a positive perspective. As in so many other situations in life, we must plan for the future. When we take the time to plan our estate, we ensure that everything we've worked for and the things we've treasured will all go to those we love. Then they can be an extension of ourselves and a final gift from us when we're no longer around.

Questions to Ask Your Parents About Their Estate

Wills and Trusts

1. Have you written and updated your will?
2. Have you written an advanced health care directive (living will)?
3. Have you created a revocable or irrevocable trust?
4. Who is the appointed estate trustee?

Beneficiary Information

5. Are all of the beneficiaries updated and ownership verified? This should include insurance, IRA, 401(k), pension, and other retirement plans.
6. Have you made pet care arrangements?

Funeral Arrangements

7. Have you written a letter of final instruction?
8. Have you prepaid for your funeral arrangements?
9. Have you designated a funeral overseer? If so, who is the funeral overseer?

Miscellaneous

10. Have you designated a financial and health care Power of Attorney?
11. Have you designated charities to receive gifts from your estates, including artwork?
12. Have you written and updated a business plan of succession?
13. The location of the following documents:
    - Will & Trust
    - Insurance policies
    - Real estate deeds

- Certificates for stocks, bonds, annuities
- Tax documents
- Letter of final instruction
- Information on bank accounts, mutual funds, and safety deposit boxes
- Information on retirement plans: 401(k), IRA, pension
- Information on debts: Credit cards, mortgages and loans, utilities, unpaid taxes, and other outstanding debts
- Information on funeral prepayment plans, power of attorney documents, and other end-of-life documents
- Password lists for websites and digital files
- Automobile/RV/boat titles

Let's Hear from the Expert

Francis K. Tennant

Francis K. Tennant is a partner in the Chicago-based law firm of Wolf & Tennant.

Nobody likes to discuss estate planning, writing a will, and the other topics that come up when planning for the eventual end of life. Everyone procrastinates and hopes to live forever. With your parents, discussing these issues may be further complicated by their understandable unwillingness to give up total control over their lives. As we age, we want to hold on to our independence, and we often express this desire by insisting on living alone and taking care of ourselves, on driving rather than being driven, and on determining who takes what we have when the time comes. Broaching these issues with an unwilling parent is not easy. A common response is, "I'm not dead yet!"

The first objective is to make sure that your parents know why you want to talk to them about their estate planning and whether they have given it any thought themselves. They need to be assured that the child is asking for the parents' benefit, not for his or her own personal gain. There might be reluctance on the part of some parents to even share information as to their assets with their children.

The conversation should begin with you making it clear that you want to make sure they have everything set-up properly so that their wishes can be clearly followed. Everyone knows a story about someone whose affairs were not in order and how everything ended in a mess. The story about the poor planners may present an opportunity to begin the discussion. Parents often want their children to be treated equally and to not show favorites. It is best for all the children to be involved in the discussion. If all the children engage with the parents in an open discussion of the parents' wishes, there will not be an opportunity for secrets, hiding information, and later problems. This may make the parents more open to having the discussion.

Discussing the effects of failing to properly plan is quite helpful. At the least, your parents should have a will and Power of Attorney for property matters, as well as a Power of Attorney for health care or other health care directives, such as a DNR order. Reviewing the need for a medical Power of Attorney is a good way to open up the discussion. Tell them why they need it: so that their wishes are known and followed. Let them know that these important documents are for their benefit as well as for the benefit of their children.

A Power of Attorney for health care is essential. This document empowers an individual to make health care decisions for the concerned party. For example, an adult child with an elderly parent might be designated by a Power of Attorney for health care to decide on medical care for their parent if the parent is unable to make the decisions herself. While health care professionals are now very attuned to the need for these documents, the family should also be aware of them and involved in their creation. They take a lot of the burden and pressure off the children because they clearly communicate a parent's medical wishes. Without direction, children are left to guess what the parent would want, especially with end-of-life decisions. The parents' direction gives the children peace of mind that they are following what the parents want, and this in turn allows the children not to agonize over whether they did the right thing in directing or withholding certain treatments. It eliminates second-guessing decisions. This also helps keep siblings from questioning the acting child's decision.

Not having the estate plan in proper form may result in many problems that can be avoided when there has been open communication with the children. I can't stress enough how important it is to review beneficiary designations. Having a beneficiary takes an asset out of probate, which means that the asset passes directly to the named beneficiary. While avoiding probate is the end result of much estate planning, it must be done right, and beneficiary designations must constantly be reviewed.

Retirement, IRA, and 401(k) accounts are owned by the individual and held with a beneficiary designation. It is important that these beneficiary designations are revised when circumstances change. When an individual names his or her spouse as the beneficiary, that designation needs to be changed if, for example, the spouse predeceases the individual. A contingent beneficiary may be named after the spouse. When no contingent beneficiary is named and the spouse has predeceased, the retirement account will pass to the individual's heirs, and this necessitates a probate. Therefore, it is essential to discuss beneficiary arrangements with parents to ensure this situation is avoided.

In order to avoid probate, parents will sometimes place assets in a joint tenancy with one of their children, with the expectation that the child will use the assets for payment of the parents' final expenses and then divide the balance among all of the children. In a perfect world this arrangement can work; however, there are several potential problems with it. First, the child is a co-owner and can take the assets during the parents' lifetime. Second, as a co-owner, the assets are subject to claims of the child's creditors. Finally, as the surviving joint tenant, the child may take the asset and not distribute any portion of it to his or her siblings.

When a parent does not execute a Power of Attorney for property and/or a Power of Attorney for health care or another health care directive, the need arises for a Guardianship. This is a court process which authorizes the guardian to make financial and health care decisions for the parent. The decisions must be approved by the Court.

This process incurs needless expenses which the Powers of Attorney are intended to avoid. In the Guardianship process, the Court must appoint a Guardian. There have been situations where competing bids by children to become the Guardian result in a hearing focused on the individual best-suited to serve. This can create divisions within the family, even when none had previously existed. The parent is best-suited to determine which of their children possess the gifts necessary to act as power of attorney.

Probate, being a court proceeding, is a matter of public record. This may not have been an important consideration in the past when someone had to go to the courthouse and look through files to obtain information about the deceased. However, in this age of the internet and open records, personal details can be found with a few keystrokes. This accessible information includes the will, of course, with its provisions for distribution of the estate. In addition, one can find names and addresses and the approximate value of the estate. An estate plan utilizing a trust will avoid probate. In that way, the foregoing information is not open to disclosure to the public.

Proper planning provides the best outcome for all involved. A trust will help the involved parties avoid probate and provide for the care and maintenance of the parent when they are unable to do so by themselves. Communication will reduce the potential for interfamily conflict. A well-defined plan will reduce the opportunities for disagreement and unnecessary expenses. Finally, it provides for peace of mind for both the parents and children.

Wrap-Up

Why You Need to Talk to Your Parents about Their Estate

1. Having a conversation with your parents about estate planning isn't a sign that you're greedy. Rather, it shows that you're responsible and want to ensure that your parents' end-of-life wishes are followed.

2. When a parent offers to leave you something in their will, graciously accept it without argument. Don't let fear of animosity between family members prevent you from allowing your parents to give you something that they want to give you. This might be your only opportunity to agree to their offer.

3. It's best to have a no-nonsense attitude when it comes to estate planning, because death is inevitable. I know that nobody wants to talk about a loved one's death, but planning ahead makes it easier for everyone. Your parents leave knowing that their affairs are in order, and children don't have to fight over assets or take the estate to probate.

4. Opening the conversation about estate planning is much easier when you've created your own estate plan. It provides an excellent way to launch a discussion about the subject.

5. Remind your parents that an estate plan is much more than simply distribution of assets. It also includes medical plans such as an advanced health care directive.

6. Make sure your parents have updated and reviewed all of their beneficiaries. These include those for insurance, IRA, 401(k), pension, and pet care.

7. Make copies of all of your parents' essential estate planning documents. It's also a good idea to have the contact information of the attorney who created them in case they are later updated. If for some reason you cannot make copies, at least know where the documents are located in the event that something happens to your parents.

Chapter 9

Don't Let Your Parents Be a Target: Protect Your Parents from Financial Abuse, Heartache, and Fraud

According to a 2015 article in *AARP*, there is "evidence that our ability to detect deception declines with age."[36] One of the unfortunate side effects of this is that senior citizens are some of the people hardest hit by crimes related to financial abuse, online dating scams, or fraudulent sales and services. The older the victim, the more likely they are to be scammed.

Elder Financial Abuse

Financial abuse is the number one crime committed against the elderly. A recent MetLife study estimates the annual dollar amount loss by victims of this crime in 2010 was just under $3 billion. Even though this is just a 12 percent increase from 2008, let's keep in mind that it's estimated only one in forty-four incidents is reported.[37] It's no wonder that senior financial abuse is being called the "crime of the 21st century."[38] Clearly this is a topic that needs to be discussed with your parents.

There are a number of red flags for potential financial abuse. It's

---

[36] Shadel, Doug, and Dudley, David. "Online Dating Scams, Fraud, and Cyber Crime - AARP." AARP. June 2015. Accessed May 13, 2016.
http://www.aarp.org/money/scams-fraud/info-2015/online-dating-scam.html

[37] "Elder Financial Exploitation." National Adult Protective Services Association. Accessed May 13, 2016.
http://www.napsa-now.org/policy-advocacy/exploitation/

[38] WISER/NAPSA: *Just the Fact*. Senior Financial Abuse. Women's Institute for a Secure Retirement. 2012. Accessed May 13, 2016.
http://www.napsa-now.org/wp-content/uploads/2013/06/Fact-Sheet-Elder-Financial-Abuse-06-13.pdf

wise to have your parents keeps an eye on their bank statements and watch for any unexpected bank withdrawals or transfers as well as unusual signatures on checks. In addition, take an inventory of personal property so that your parents know what valuables they possess and where these are located. When hiring caregivers, it's important to do a background check, contact references, and verify credentials.

It's difficult to believe, but 90 percent of abusers are family members or other trusted individuals. The crimes range from outright theft of possessions to forging documents, fraudulent credit card use, and Power of Attorney abuse.

Jeanette's Story

A long-time friend of mine, "Jeanette," was single, in her late-thirties, and had just about given up hope of ever finding her Prince Charming until she met and married a very wealthy man, "Tom." Tom was nearly twenty years older than Jeanette. Recently divorced with two adult children who had graduated from college, Tom was as excited as Jeanette about finding true love. They absolutely doted on each other.

They had been married twenty-five years when Tom was diagnosed with cancer. A wise businessman, Tom had designed his will so that his children would receive a portion of the estate, but most importantly he wanted to ensure that Jeanette was very well-cared for and could maintain the lifestyle they had been living. He didn't want the woman he deeply loved to ever worry about money.

However, while Tom was in the hospital, his children showed up with a revised will. As Tom was approaching the end of his life, his kids coerced him into signing the new will, which left nearly everything to them and only a small portion of the estate to his wife.

Jeanette's life was greatly impacted by this form of senior financial abuse. She was forced to leave the home she and Tom had built and was now living on a limited income at a time in her life when she should have been preparing for retirement. Most importantly,

Tom's intentions and wishes weren't carried out due to the deception.

Elizabeth's Story

Elder financial abuse is particularly prevalent among those who are critically ill or those who have cognitive impairment either from disease or medication. These vulnerable victims can be coerced into signing financial documents and handing over assets. Seniors with Alzheimer's or dementia are especially at risk for this abuse because they can rarely recall the incidents.

A friend, "Elizabeth," had been married to her husband, "Jim," for thirty years. During this time, Jim was diagnosed with leukemia. Elizabeth was very devoted to Jim and had been his full-time caregiver through his illness. When he required more intensive care than she could handle, Elizabeth finally broke down and agreed to hire a live-in caregiver.

Everything was going well until a few weeks after hiring a forty-something nurse, at which point Elizabeth discovered the nurse wearing nothing but a robe while in her husband's room. Elizabeth was taken aback, but it wasn't until the next day when she arrived home to find the nurse and her husband in a compromising sexual position that she fully understood what was happening. With no time to argue or ask questions, Jim informed his wife that he wanted a divorce and asked her to leave. He had been on excessive amounts of pain medication at the time; it would have been difficult to believe that Jim could possibly do anything like this had he not been ill and cognitively impaired.

Elizabeth had spent a significant portion of her life caring for and loving Jim, and in the span of less than a month, she had been replaced by this nurse. Never once during their marriage had Elizabeth been involved with the family's finances. She was totally clueless about her husband's insurance and estate planning. As a result, not only had Jim kicked Elizabeth out of their home, but he had also signed papers leaving his entire estate to the nurse. Despite her taking legal action, Elizabeth walked away from her marriage with next to nothing.

Let's Talk about Senior Financial Abuse

Protecting your parents from this type of abuse requires not just discussion, but observation of your parents' habits and behaviors as well. Changes in a parent's mood can signal a problem. Anxiety about finances and a change in banking habits can be reasons for concern. Further, uneasiness when discussing the topic is yet another red flag.

Depending on your parent's cognitive skills, this can be a difficult topic to bring up. Nobody wants to think they've been taken advantage of, but when your memory is declining, it's an even more painful discovery. It's embarrassing to admit that you've been swindled by a family member or someone you trusted. This is one reason the crime is underreported.

Your parents might also feel intimidated or afraid to discuss the situation. Before his death, actor Mickey Rooney testified before a Senate Special Committee on Aging about his personal experience with this form of abuse. Prior to giving testimony, Rooney was granted a temporary protection order because he was afraid of his alleged abusers: his stepson and daughter-in-law.[39]

Letting your parents know that they can confide in you without judgement is one of the best ways to get them to open up about possible financial abuse. Listen with an open heart and assure them they're not alone. There are numerous resources available for victims, including the National Committee for the Prevention of Elder Abuse, Eldercare, the National Crime Prevention Council, Adult Protective Services, and local branches of Area Agency on Aging.

Protecting Your Parents Online: Dating Scams

While your parents are probably savvy enough not to be

---

[39] Gjertsen II, Ed. "The 'double life' of Mickey Rooney." CNBC. April 10, 2014. Accessed May 13, 2016.
http://www.cnbc.com/2014/04/10/the-double-life-of-mickey-rooney.html.

scammed by emails from Ethiopia asking them to wire $10,000 in order to receive a $1,000,000 inheritance, let me assure you, there are many more ways for people to take advantage of the elderly online.

The death or divorce of a long-term spouse can be devastating regardless of your age. Due to the loneliness one feels from the loss of a partner, along with the sense of isolation and the need to be loved again, one of the most prevalent crimes among those who are divorced or widowed is online dating scams.

The $2.2 billion online dating industry is an integral part of our culture. Almost 14 percent of users are of retirement age,[40] and online dating scams have become so prevalent that the FBI has a website page highlighting the warning signs of this crime.[41] In 2014, the Internet Crime Complaint Center (IC3) reported nearly 5,900 cases of online dating scams, costing victims more than $86.7 million dollars.[42] And much like senior financial abuse, many cases go unreported, so it's difficult to know the full extent of these scams.

While both sexes of every age group are susceptible to online dating fraud, scammers tend to target women over forty.[43] An average of $15,000 to $20,000 per relationship is lost,[44] but it's not

[40] Harwell, Drew. "Online Dating's Age Wars: Inside Tinder and eHarmony's Fight for Our Love Lives." Washington Post. April 6, 2015. Accessed May 13, 2016.
https://www.washingtonpost.com/news/business/wp/2015/04/06/online-datings-age-wars-inside-tinder-and-eharmonys-fight-for-our-love-lives/
[41] Federal Bureau of Investigation. "Looking for Love? Beware of Online Dating Scams." February 14, 2012. Accessed May 13, 2016.
https://www.fbi.gov/news/stories/2012/february/dating-scams_021412
[42] Abramo, Allegra. "Dating-site Scammers Tear up Hearts, Empty Wallets." CNBC. August 06, 2015. Accessed May 13, 2016.
http://www.cnbc.com/2015/08/06/dating-site-scammers-tear-up-hearts-empty-wallets.html.
[43] Federal Bureau of Investigation. "Looking for Love? Beware of Online Dating Scams." February 14, 2012. Accessed May 13, 2016.
https://www.fbi.gov/news/stories/2012/february/dating-scams_021412
[44] Federal Bureau of Investigation. "Sweetheart Scams." February 14, 2012. Accessed May 13, 2016.
https://www.fbi.gov/news/stories/2012/february/dating-scams_021412

uncommon for those taken by this con to be swindled out of their life savings and lose everything they own.

According to the FBI, there are quite a few red flags that the handsome, graying man from Minnesota that your mother is corresponding with is actually a Nigerian, twenty-something internet con artist. These warning signs include:

- The declaration of love soon after making contact.
- Photos that appear to be "too good to be true."
- The suitor claims to be living abroad for work or travel.
- He or she expresses a desire to visit but can't afford the plane ticket.
- He or she asks for money for any reason, but especially a sob story about medical expenses, emergencies, and other excuses to tug at your heart strings.[45]

The Anatomy of an Online Dating Scam

Common sense can sometimes take a back seat when the heart is involved. But you have to hand it to the online dating scammers as well, because they're pretty slick. After setting up a fake social media or dating site profile, the con artist will often contact victims with flattering messages, such as, "You're the woman of my dreams." The next thing you know you're invited to Yahoo messenger or another social media messaging app to get you away from your original meeting place, and to keep your conversation away from the dating service. And the scam doesn't always take place quickly; scammers can take their time building up trust with their potential victims.

Although there's always some reason you can't see each other in person on Skype, he'll flood your in-box with messages declaring his love for you with reminders of how much you mean to him. He'll ask you questions about your personal life in order to achieve a new

---

[45] Federal Bureau of Investigation. "Looking for Love? Beware of Online Dating Scams." February 9, 2012. Accessed May 13, 2016.
https://www.fbi.gov/news/podcasts/inside/sweetheart-scams.mp3/view

level of trust and intimacy in your relationship. In some cases, he might ask you to send compromising photos or videos.

And then, suddenly, BAM! For some reason he can't access his bank account and really needs your help. He'll either ask you for a small loan to help him out or have some solution that involves sending you to the bank. Shortly after this, you can count on a serious calamity. It might be a medical emergency for his daughter that he can't afford or the intense desire to visit you, but again, he lacks funds. And after that problem has been solved with you wiring money to him, I assure you, there will be another major disaster . . . and another . . . and another . . . until you've depleted your savings, emptied retirement accounts, sold your assets; you name it, he'll take it.

And then he'll leave.

Not only will your online romance leave you penniless, but it will also leave you broken-hearted. It's surprising that even after discovering their lover is a fraud, many women (and men) want to return to the relationship. Fortunately, there are support groups, such as RomanceScams.org and LooksTooGoodToBeTrue.com. Both of these websites provide counseling, along with information on how to identify and report the crime and useful links, such as those for IC3, Western Union, and the U.S. Secret Service.

If a parent has fallen for an online dating scam, try to get help for them and provide as much emotional support as possible. This is a difficult and painful crime for its victims. The last thing your parent needs to hear is how stupid he or she was for being taken in by a scammer.

The Vulnerable Widower

The internet isn't the only dangerous place for your senior, partner-less parent. Interestingly, widowed men find the loss of a loved one more emotionally difficult, and as a result, they're nearly ten times more likely to remarry than widowed women.[46] Not only that, but men rarely wait long to remarry after the death of their beloved wives.

A widower left with a decent nest egg after his wife's passing can quickly become a target for younger women eager to fill the void. Lured by the attention of an attractive woman and the desire for companionship, a lonely widower can easily be enticed to suddenly jump into a new marriage with or without his children's consent.

If your widowed parent decides to date again, be aware that you will most likely experience some conflicting emotions. There's a fine line between mourning the loss of the parent that passed away and wanting your living parent to be happy. While children want their parents to be content, there can sometimes be a very steep cost for this joy.

Nicole's Story

A client, "Nicole," was very close to her childless godmother, "Virginia." Although her godparents lived in Connecticut, she spoke to her godmother daily and sent cards to her on a weekly basis. Having lost both her parents earlier in her life, Nicole thought of and treated her godparents as her own parents.

Virginia had worked hard her entire life and saved religiously. She wanted to ensure that she'd leave a substantial amount of money to her goddaughter after she passed away. She frequently told Nicole that her estate would one day belong to her.

Virginia unexpectedly became critically ill. Nicole immediately made plans to visit her godmother in the hospital, but her godfather informed Nicole that Virginia didn't want visitors—that she didn't want Nicole to see her in such a sickly condition. This saddened Nicole greatly, but she honored her godmother's wishes.

Nicole received the phone call informing her of Virginia's death

---

[46] "Marriage & Remarriage." Marriage & Remarriage. 2009. Accessed May 13, 2016. http://www.nap411.com/family/family-diversity/marriage-a-remarriage

several weeks later. She returned to her godparents' home and consoled her grieving godfather. At this time, her godfather reminded Nicole that she was the sole beneficiary of their estate when he passed away, and that she would be the estate's trustee. Nicole was too grief-stricken to pay much attention or request paperwork, but she thanked her godfather and told him that she would take care of the estate when the time came.

It was about six months after Virginia's death when Nicole's godfather called to tell Nicole about his new girlfriend. When pushed for details, he confessed that he had gotten married a few days earlier. He sounded elated when he informed her of his marriage to "Jiao." It was not a formal wedding or anything—just a couple of friends as witnesses at the courthouse. Nicole was devastated by the news. She was deeply hurt that her godfather hadn't introduced her to his bride or included her in the wedding, but she didn't want to spoil her godfather's bliss. Although Nicole hadn't had a chance to meet Jiao, she had heard from friends that Jiao was a fairly young Chinese woman who spoke very little English. Nicole was stunned after receiving a photograph of her godfather with his new bride; Jiao appeared to be younger than herself. Nicole tried to be supportive when she called to check on her godfather every week, always asking how Jiao was, but she never had a desire to meet the woman who had quickly taken her godmother's place.

Less than a year later, Nicole's godfather suffered a fatal heart attack. Hearing the news from a friend, Nicole attempted to contact Jiao to discuss her godfather's burial, but she was unable to reach her. Nicole had no way to contact Jiao because Jiao's English was so limited. Nicole was never contacted about funeral arrangements or even invited to the service.

Several days after the funeral, Nicole received a phone call from an attorney claiming to be the trustee for her godfather's estate. Nicole was baffled by this information because she assumed that she was the trustee. Apparently, her godfather had changed all of his estate planning after marrying Jiao. He had appointed a local attorney as trustee and left everything except the funds in his checking account to his new bride. After paying for the funeral and other expenses, Nicole was left with absolutely nothing. In fact, she wasn't even allowed to take photos or any of her beloved godmother's possessions out of the house because they were included in Jiao's inheritance. Nicole was heartbroken.

Nicole's story is not unique. If your mother, father, or relatives express a desire to leave you a set amount of assets or family heirlooms, make sure these requests are irrevocable in their estate planning. Nicole's godmother probably never anticipated her husband remarrying after her death, but I'm sure if she had considered this, she would have protected her goddaughter. Nicole not only lost a sizeable inheritance and all of her godmother's treasures, but most importantly, her godmother's wishes weren't granted.

Here's the thing: you never know if your widowed or divorced parent is going to find love again, and let me tell you, remarriage is a game-changer when it comes to estate planning. In most states, assets transfer directly to the spouse. It doesn't matter if your dad was married to his new wife for ten years or ten months—properties transfer to his spouse. Insist that your parents protect their assets *before* they die by creating irrevocable trusts. Doing this not only ensures you get what your parents want you to have, but it also offers excellent tax advantages.

Let's Talk about Love and our Single Parent

Regardless of whether your divorced or widowed parent meets a new love interest online or in person, you want to make sure they make smart financial decisions in the relationship. Love can sometimes play havoc with common sense. This is why it's critical that you ask questions to ensure your loved one sees any flaws in their reasoning.

Online dating scams play to the most vulnerable. The elderly (well, *all* of us at one time or another) can have a need for attention that is overwhelming, and which creates a hunger. Messages and emails from an ardent admirer declaring love and attraction flood the veins of victims like a drug. Breaking loose from a scammer is often incredibly painful. In fact, many people want to return to the relationship even after their "lover" has been proven to be a criminal. I caution you to seek professional assistance as you begin the conversation about breaking free from a fraudulent online romance.

However, should you believe your parent is involved in a fake relationship, you can certainly ask questions to help confirm or disprove your suspicions. Look for discrepancies in information and point out illogical parts of the person's story. Of course, if your parent is already besotted with the possible scammer, be prepared to face opposition and excuses for why there is conflicting or confusing information. At the very least, though, bringing up concerns plants a seed for future contemplation.

You know the old saying, "If it sounds too good to be true, it probably is." Well, if your eighty-something father is dating a woman half his age, I would definitely have a chat about the age difference and what they have in common. After all, you're his daughter, and you should be interested in who your father is dating. It can be a real bonding moment between the two of you—a sort of role reversal. To help lighten the mood when talking to your dad, mention the times he scrutinized *your* boyfriends. Just letting him know that you don't want him to get hurt can mean so much, and can open the door to the conversation.

Questions to Ask to Protect Your Parents from Financial Abuse and Fraud

Financial Abuse

1. Have you or your parents seen any unexpected bank withdrawals or transfers between accounts?
2. Are you or your parents aware of any personal property missing?
3. Have you or your parents noticed any unusual signatures on checks?
4. Have any new caregivers been hired? If so, what are their credentials and do they come from a reputable agency?

Online Dating Fraud

5. Does the person seem "too good to be true"?
6. Does the person currently live outside the United States?
7. Has the person asked for money or mentioned a need for money? Have you sent any money?
8. Did the person contact you? If so, how long did it take for him/her to tell you that he/she loves you?

Dating

9. How did you meet?
10. How old is your new partner?
11. Does your new partner have children? If so, how many and how old?
12. What does your new partner do for a living?

General

13. Do you have documentation regarding your parents' wills?
14. Have their wills changed since they met their new partner?
15. Have they created irrevocable trusts?

Let's Hear from the Expert

Benjamin W. Wong

Benjamin W. Wong is with the Lincoln Park law firm of Benjamin W. Wong & Associates, Ltd. He focuses his practice on estate planning, estate and trust administration, and real estate.

What can I do to protect my elderly parents from financial abuse?

The elderly can be easy targets for financial abuse, especially identity theft. To avoid falling victim to fraudsters, your elderly parents can follow these basic tips:

- Buy a shredder to shred important information and keep it out of the hands of thieves.
- It may go without saying, but they should not respond to cold phone calls or emails requesting personal information, such as social security numbers, passwords or PINs.
- Credit reports should be checked regularly for suspicious activity.
- Check their mail regularly, especially when waiting for important documents.
- Have their phone number unlisted and/or put their phone number on the Do Not Call Registry.

What warning signs should I be on the lookout for indicating that my elderly parents may be susceptible to financial abuse?

Your parents' cognitive abilities should be closely monitored. Judgment and critical thinking skills tend to deteriorate over time, especially for those in their eighties and nineties. One warning sign is that their spending habits suddenly change. For example, if they are normally frugal in their spending but start making major purchases, this could be a warning sign that their mental faculties are deteriorating. Also, if your parents are lonely, they may be susceptible to being charmed by fraudsters who are good at cultivating relationships. It is important to be aware of any new people who want to befriend your parents.

If I suspect that my parents have been victims of financial abuse, what should I do?

If your parents are victims of financial abuse, the authorities should be called. Many states have state-operated social service agencies that are responsible for investigating the abuse, neglect or exploitation of the elderly.

What estate planning documents do my elderly parents need?

A trust should be set up. It is a legal mechanism in which one person, called a trustee, manages the property on behalf of another person, called the beneficiary. The trust is the owner of the property and the beneficiary is the person who receives the benefits of the trust property. Having a dependable and trustworthy trustee can help protect your parents' assets.

A power of attorney should be prepared. A Power of Attorney for Property will allow your parents to appoint an agent who can act for them in order to handle their financial affairs. The reason it is important to create a Power of Attorney for Property is to ensure that if, for any reason, your parents are incapable of handling their own financial affairs due to accident, illness, or unavailability, the person they name (their agent) can step in and handle these matters for them.

What can I do to help after the death of one of my parents?

The first thing you can help your remaining parent do is make sure they have their financial support team together. This includes an estate planning attorney, an accountant, a financial advisor, and an insurance professional. These trusted professionals will help you protect your parents' assets for years to come. The estate planning attorney can update the new heirs in an existing will. The accountant can prepare taxes. The financial advisor can make sure investments are allocated properly and can assist in rolling over the spouse's retirement accounts. The life insurance agent can assist in filing life insurance claims so that insurance proceeds can be accessed as soon as possible.

When should my widowed parent start making major financial decisions?

It's highly recommended to wait six months to a year before making any major financial decisions after the loss of a spouse. Emotions typically run high during the grieving process, and your parent may not be in the right frame of mind to think clearly. As time passes, your parent will be able to be more objective and make the best financial decisions possible. For example, your parent should not rush into buying or selling investments they do not completely understand. If they receive a large life insurance death benefit, it is best to invest it conservatively, such as in a money market account, and then wait until they are ready to make an informed, educated decision.

What should I do if my parent starts dating again?

If your parent starts dating again, you need to be aware that your parent's potential partner may be looking for spending money. You should warn your parent to keep money matters private until they feel entirely sure the new partner is trustworthy. At a minimum, your parent needs to know that the new partner's intentions are not financially-related. As their child, you can make yourself available to discuss these issues with your parent.

My parent has a house and no one to share it with. What should she do with it?

Some widows stay in their house and rush to pay off their mortgage with the life insurance death benefits. Your parent should wait to pay off the mortgage, or at least consider the option carefully, because the influx of cash from, for example, a life insurance policy, can also be used for short-term needs. Have your parent take time to evaluate what those needs truly are, especially because they may change with the passing of their spouse. Other widows, on the other hand, rush to sell their home and move in with family members to escape the emptiness of an empty home and a lost spouse. Sometimes this necessitates moving to a different part of the country. It is always possible that the feeling of loneliness will subside, and then the parent must deal with what can be an equally traumatic sense of loss at having left behind a social network and daily routine. Whatever decision your parent makes, make sure they carefully think it through, and offer to help them do so.

Wrap-Up

Why You Need to Protect Your Parents from Financial Abuse and Fraud

1. Financial abuse is the number one crime against the elderly. The offender is often a relative or someone trusted by the victim. The crimes can include theft of possessions, forging documents, fraudulent credit card use, and Power of Attorney abuse.

2. Red flags that your parent might be suffering from financial abuse include: anxiety about money, sudden bank withdrawals or money transfers, and a reluctance to discuss the subject.

3. Lonely, widowed or divorced seniors are easy targets for online dating predators. If a person seems "too good to be true," then he is most likely a scammer.

4. Victims of online dating scams suffer both financially and emotionally. Great care must be taken to help the victim heal. Seek professional assistance to help with the psychological impact of being an online dating victim.

5. Whether your parent meets someone online or in person, make sure your parent's net worth isn't the reason for the relationship.

6. Make sure a parent or relative wanting to leave you a part of their estate creates an irrevocable trust in order to protect what they want to leave you. Remarriage is a game-changer when it comes to estate planning. Protect your parents' wishes and your future inheritance.

Let's Talk about Retirement

*Not having a financial plan is a plan—it's
a really bad plan.*

Alexa Van Tobel

Chapter 10

IRA, 401(k), SEP ... It's all Greek to Me: Make Sense of Your Retirement Savings Plans

W e all learned the ABC song when we were children, but nobody thought to explain the ABCs of retirement when we grew up. If you've ever met with a financial planner, you probably heard cryptic mentions of IRAs, SEPs, 401(k)s, or ESOPs and wondered what language was being spoken. Learning the retirement alphabet isn't as difficult as most people think, but it's an important vocabulary to acquire.

Retirement Plans at a Glance

If you're receiving retirement benefits from your employer, chances are very likely that you're already in a retirement plan. However, it's wise to know what plans are available to ensure you're putting your money where it can grow the most.

When I discuss retirement plans with clients, I like to use the analogy of bowls. There is a 401(k) bowl, an IRA bowl, an IRA Roth bowl, a SEP bowl, and so on. The key is to determine which bowls you want to fill up. Your ultimate goal is to balance these bowls so that there aren't too many or too few risks. Let's talk a little about some of the bowls you can choose from.

The retirement plan offered by most employers is the 401(k) or 403(b). Contributions to these plans are often withheld from your paycheck and matched by your employer, and you're currently allowed to contribute up to $18,000 to them annually. If you're fifty or over, you can bump that pre-tax contribution to $24,000.

Although you can certainly increase that amount, be aware that it will not be pre-tax. Plus, you'll want to work closely with your financial advisor to strategize so that the increase won't bump you into the next tax bracket when you hit retirement age. One of the best features of a 401(k) or 403(b) is that they can easily be rolled over should you change employers.

Probably one of the most intimidating aspects of the 401(k) and 403(b) is that you're required to choose the investments for your plan. There are a variety of funds to choose from for this bowl. Depending on the age when you started planning and your retirement goals, you'll want to look at the risk factor of each investment. If you're nearing retirement, now is not the time to take enormous risks. That said, you don't want to stay *too* safe either. Your employer-sponsored 401(k) or 403(b) account often comes with financial services to advise you on your investment portfolio. If you're not working with a financial advisor, make sure you take advantage of this free service to ensure your retirement savings are in the most effective funds.

The other retirement plan you've most likely heard about is the Individual Retirement Account (IRA). IRAs are a little trickier because there are lots of IRA bowls to choose from. For example, there is your traditional IRA, but there is also the Roth IRA, Savings Incentive Match Plans for Employees (SIMPLE) IRA, Simplified Employee Pension (SEP) IRA, Salary Reduction Simplified Employee Pension (SARSEP) IRA, and Payroll Deduction IRA. Each plan offers certain features and has specific stipulations regarding taxes and withdrawals. It's best to consult with a financial professional to ensure you're making the best decision before you put your money into any of these bowls.

Some employers offer an opportunity to save money tax-free in a Health Savings Account (HSA). An HSA is geared toward those with a high-deductible health insurance plan, but it's also handy to use when paying for medical expenses, including dental and optometry services. Individuals under fifty-five can currently contribute as much as $3,350 per year pre-tax, while those over fifty-five can add another $1,000 to the fund. Families can sock away as much as $6,650 each year. Although some HSA plans require you to spend the entire amount within the calendar year, others will allow you to roll over your unused balance from year-to-year. With these plans, you either use the funds for medical expenses or invest them in another retirement savings plan without penalty until you turn sixty-five.

In addition to the plans discussed above, those of you who are self-employed or own a small business have additional bowls for your retirement savings. The Simplified Employee Pension (SEP) IRA is often used by those who own a business with less than one hundred employees. An SEP IRA is fairly easy to establish for your employees and allows you to contribute up to twenty-five percent of your annual income if you're the business owner.

The Solo 401(k) is for business owners without employees. The beauty of the Solo 401(k) is that it covers the business owner and their spouse. There's no need to follow the complicated Employee Retirement Income Security Act of 1974 (ERISA) guidelines for employer contributions because you don't have any employees to cover. Those who qualify for a Solo 401(k) are eligible for the same tax benefits of those with an individual 401(k).

Filling the Bowls

Now that you have a better idea about what bowls are available for your retirement planning, it's time to start filling them. While you select your bowls, you want to consider the three types of distributions for your funds—tax-free, tax-deferred, or taxable. This is important, because you will want to strategically plan your retirement savings distribution. Between the ages of twenty to sixty, you're an *income generator*, but once you hit your sixties, you become an *income distributor*, and you want to make sure you distribute your savings wisely.

The investments you fill your bowls with should be chosen carefully. Remember, I want you to create balanced bowls. This means that you're going to include some reliable, but low income-producing investments along with some slightly riskier ones. The younger you are, the riskier you can be, but always diversify and keep those bowls balanced. You need to know how much risk you're taking for the growth of your money. Seek the advice of a financial professional if you're unsure of an investment's performance and risk.

Planning your retirement isn't an onerous task. Using a retirement analyzer that looks at your current financial situation, a financial professional can help ensure that your bowls are balanced with investments that will make your money grow. Remember, there aren't any scholarships for retirement, so you have to make sure you save wisely and enlist the assistance of those who can advise you to make the best choices. You can only increase your retirement savings by putting more money away, working longer, or my personal favorite—making your money work for you.

The Magic Number is 70 ½

There's one thing for certain about retirement—Uncle Sam wants you to retire. Even if you don't need the extra income from your 401(k) or other retirement plans, you're required by the IRS to receive at least the minimum distribution from all of your retirement accounts when you turn 70 ½ years old. The exception to this rule is the Roth IRA, which doesn't have to be disbursed until after your death.

Trust me when I tell you that the IRS is serious about this requirement—I'm not exaggerating. Uncle Sam has very strict guidelines for the Required Minimum Distribution (RMD) based on your life expectancy.[47] Using the Uniform Lifetime Table, someone who is seventy years old is expected to live an additional 27.4 years. While this seems optimistic, the IRS wants to guarantee you'll have sufficient funds to make it to ripe old age of 97.4. This means your RMD will be approximately 3.65 percent of your IRA balance.

Although you can withdraw more money than the RMD, keep in mind that most funds will be taxed and counted as income. This is

---

[47] "IRA Required Minimum Distribution Worksheet." Accessed May 13, 2016. https://www.irs.gov/pub/irs-tege/uniform_rmd_wksht.pdf

something to consider as you plan your retirement. You want to make sure your RMD doesn't throw you into a higher tax bracket. A financial professional, such as a Chartered Retirement Planning Counselor, can help you strategize your distributions in order to pay fewer taxes on your investments.

Patricia's Story

"Patricia" had been a loyal client for over two decades. Patricia began saving for retirement as soon as she returned to work after the birth of her first child. Her parents stressed the importance of planning early for retirement, and she listened carefully to their warnings. She retired several years ago but had budgeted and planned so well that she hesitated withdrawing funds from her retirement accounts. As she approached the magical age of 70 ½, she wanted to make sure she didn't have to pay the enormous fifty percent tax penalty, but she also didn't want to get bumped into a higher tax bracket.

Patricia had reason for concern because she was absolutely correct. If she took her RMD, she would move into the next tax bracket and pay considerably more to Uncle Sam. I suggested Patricia convert her taxable IRA into tax-free life insurance. This would protect Patricia's savings, and in the event of her death, it would provide tax-free money to her beneficiaries.

There are other tax-free options available for those who find themselves in Patricia's situation. Rather than accept that you'll have to pay more taxes, talk to a financial professional and ask questions. Remember, don't settle for less.

Navigating the labyrinth of retirement options can certainly seem intimidating, but with guidance from a retirement professional, you'll soon understand enough to feel confident discussing and making decisions about your retirement plan. While the best options will vary from person to person, it's worth making the effort to get informed and become empowered about these important issues, so start talking. Speak up and let your voice be heard!

Financial Questions to Ask About Retirement Plans

1. What are some strategies to avoid paying taxes on my retirement savings?

2. What retirement plans allow the greatest contribution amounts?

3. Are there other types of retirement accounts available to me that offer different kinds of benefits?

4. Do I qualify to contribute to more than one type of retirement account?

5. What types of retirement plans best suit my needs? What bowls should I fill up?

6. What is the return on my investments?

7. What investments should I choose?

8. How do I know if my bowls are balanced?

9. Will the distributions be taxable, tax-deferred, or tax-free?

Let's Hear from the Expert

Cory Goldman, CRPC

Cory Goldman is a Northern Illinois University graduate and has completed the CFP™ coursework through Northwestern University. In 2015 Cory obtained his CRPC® designation and became a Chartered Retirement Plan Consultant.

Make sense of your retirement savings plan

After seven years in the financial industry, I've had the chance to hear many people's thoughts on how to save for retirement. A remark I often get is, "I hear you need $1,000,000 to retire." Let's go over the dangers of subscribing to a retirement game plan like this and see what questions you *really* need to ask.

When will you retire?

As we all *should* know, the average price of goods and services rises every year. This phenomenon is called inflation. In 1995 the average price of a movie ticket was $4.35. Today, that same ticket goes for $8.70. Exactly double. So if you planned to have $1,000,000 for when you retire, the real question becomes how much stuff can that $1,000,000 buy you in the year you plan to retire. Maybe it's not enough.

What are your plans for your retirement lifestyle?

The cost of retirement is not fixed. When we retire, we don't go to the retirement store and take a retirement off the shelves and go to the checkout register. It sounds like a silly thing to say, but it's making an important point. How you plan on spending your golden years dictates the price tag your retirement plans will carry. Plan on traveling the world? Account for it. Plan on moving to a warmer climate? Account for it. Plan on living modestly? Accou— You get the idea. $1,000,000 may not cover what you had in mind for yourself, *especially* if your retirement is ten-plus years away.

Recreating your income in retirement

Now that we know how much our retirement will cost, it's time to recreate our income. Since we no longer have income from employment, we have to look elsewhere to recreate the income that will support the lifestyle we planned. For the majority of us, most, if not all of this income will come from Social Security and our savings. We can get a relatively accurate forecast of these numbers years, even decades in advance. This allows us the ability to effectively save in a manner that matches our retirement plans.

Wrap-Up

Why You Need to Understand the Different Retirement Plans

1. Don't be intimidated by the retirement alphabet. Learn the vocabulary to ensure you're putting your money where it can grow.

2. When planning your retirement, think about putting your money in different bowls. The different bowls include 401(k), 403(b), IRA, Roth IRA, SIMPLE IRA, SEP IRA, SARSEP IRA, Payroll Deduction IRA, HSA, Profit-Sharing Plans, Defined Benefit Plans, Money Purchase Plans, and ESOPs.

3. The key to successful retirement planning is to have balanced bowls—diversify your options.

4. When choosing investments, consider the three types of distributions: tax-free, tax-deferred, and taxable. After you retire, you will want to strategize how you receive these different types of funds.

5. There aren't any scholarships for retirement, so you have to make sure you save wisely and enlist the assistance of those who can advise you to make the best choices.

6. When choosing investments, look for a variety of reliable as well as riskier choices. You want your money to work for you.

7. The magic retirement distribution number is 70½. The IRS requires you to receive the minimum distribution when you turn 70½ years old.

8. Failing to take your Required Minimum Distribution (RMD) when you turn 70½ will result in a 50 percent tax penalty.

9. You're allowed to withdraw more than the RMD, but be careful not to withdraw so much that you move into a higher tax bracket.

10. There are tax-free options for those who find themselves in a higher tax bracket after the RMD.

Chapter 11

It's Never Too Soon to Start Planning: Plan Early for a Sunny Retirement

I realize it's cliché to use the old adage about the early bird getting the worm when talking about retirement savings, but the fact is, it's absolutely true. The sooner you begin putting money into a retirement plan, the more wealth you're going to accumulate.

Put Your Money to Work

I'm always a little surprised when younger clients tell me that they can't afford to invest money. This is when I tell them that they can't afford *not* to invest their money. The truth is, the earlier you begin investing your money, the larger that investment will grow. Instead of working harder to earn more money, I urge you to make your money do the work. Let me show you how.

A friend was talking to me the other day about her seventeen-year-old daughter. When she told me that her daughter had just gotten a summer job at their neighborhood pool, I instinctively advised her to encourage her daughter to start investing her money. My friend laughed and looked puzzled that a teenager should consider a retirement plan. That's when I launched in on the tax benefits of retirement savings, as well as the miracle of compound interest.

Compound Interest

When we speak of "interest," we're referring to a periodic cash distribution from an investment. The term "compound" tells us these distributions are being *reinvested*, usually back into the same investment.

And let me tell you—compound interest is the eighth wonder of the world, girlfriends. It's the magic that helps your money grow. Essentially, compound interest is interest that's added to the principal of your initial investment. Every year when your investment earns interest, that interest is added to the principal. This means the added interest also gains interest. It's like a BOGO (buy-one-get-one-free) on interest!

If a compound interest investment makes periodic cash distributions, as the investor, you have two options: reinvest the cash distribution (a.k.a. interest) giving you additional shares, or not reinvest, and your cash distributions remain as cash.

Some common types of investments that allow us to benefit from compound interest are: dividend paying stocks, dividend paying mutual funds, and exchange-traded funds. If you wish to benefit from compound interest, contact the institution where your investment is or will be held, and make sure your investment(s) are reinvesting.

When talking about compound interest, it's important to make the distinction between an "account" and an "investment." We can compare the differences of an "account" and an "investment" just as we can compare the differences between a "bowl" and "a thing that can be held in a bowl." An account is a "bowl" while an investment is "a thing that can be held in a bowl."

Accounts don't offer compound interest; *certain investments* offer compound interest. It is very common to have an account that contains investments that offer compound interest and investments that don't. If an investment makes periodic cash distributions and offers you the option to reinvest the distributions, it is a compound interest investment. Growth stocks don't typically pay dividends.

Plus, it's very important to understand that simply because an investment allows for dividend reinvestment, it doesn't necessarily mean it will yield a higher return. The take-home message about compound interest and investing is to keep your money invested. This includes the distributions that investments sometimes earn.

Let's say I'm my friend's daughter and I put $5,000 into a compound interest investment earning 5 percent annual interest. If I don't reinvest the interest I earn each year, I know my investment will grow by exactly $250 each year; we call this *simple interest.* However, because I'm a smart investor, I elect to continually reinvest my interest. By doing this, I earn 5 percent on a larger and larger amount each year—*compound interest.* The difference? Using simple interest, my $5,000 investment grows to $11,250 when I retire in 25 years. By reinvesting my interest and leveraging compound interest, the same investment grows to $16,932; a difference greater than my entire initial investment.

My friends, *that* is what I call making your money work for you! It's no wonder Einstein supposedly called compound interest the "greatest mathematical discovery of all time."

Now let's look at the difference between simple and compound interests from a retirement-savings perspective. Money that's invested in a simple interest account will earn considerably less because the interest isn't reinvested. If an investor puts $100,000 into an 8 percent simple interest account today and keeps it there for twenty years, the future total of that investment will be $260,000. However, a compound interest investment allows the investor to continuously reinvest the interest. If the same investor had put her $100,000 into an 8 percent compound interest account instead of a simple interest one, she'd have $466,096. That's quite a difference. And the key to the magic of compound interest is one thing: *time*! The sooner you begin putting your money to work, the more money it will produce.

My Future's So Bright, I Gotta Wear Shades

I advocate opening your first retirement account as soon as you land your first job—even if it's a part-time one. But it's absolutely crucial you start saving when you get your first full-time job. When you're young, time is your best friend. Time allows your money to grow longer. I've worked with clients who began saving for retirement when they were in their forties, and not only did they have to work harder and invest more, but they ended up with considerably less money than those who started saving when they were in their twenties.

Angela's Story

"Angela" had been referred to me by her twin brother, "Matthew," a client who began working with me when he got his first job at age twenty-five. Matthew was concerned because his thirty-five-year-old sister hadn't started saving for her retirement yet. I immediately had Angela put $5,000 per year into the same 8 percent interest-bearing account that I'd put her brother's money into ten years earlier. Although Matthew was no longer contributing to this account, his money was still growing. When the twins reached their forty-fifth birthday, they had both made the same number of contributions to their account. However, Angela's account was considerably less. Matthew's account had accumulated $194,056 while Angela's had only $89,886. Matthew hadn't invested in this account since his thirty-fifth birthday while Angela will continue to make contributions until she turns sixty. At that point, Angela will have invested $130,000 in twenty-five years. Her retirement nest egg will be $431,754. Want to know how Matthew fared? Remember, he only made payments for ten years to the tune of $55,000. His account will have a retirement value of $615,580. Now do you see why the early bird gets the worm?

I've said it before and I'll say it again: there are only three ways to increase your retirement savings. You can either put more money away, work longer, or make your money work for you. By starting your savings early, your money has more time to do the work—so you don't have to.

I'm Late, I'm Late for a Very Important Date

You're not alone if you've procrastinated saving for retirement. According to a study released by the Schwartz Center for Economic Policy Analysis at the New School, social security benefits are the only retirement plan for 55 percent of households with the head of house approaching retirement age.[48] In 2011, 68 percent of the working-age population didn't participate in an employer-sponsored retirement plan.[49] Furthermore, many who do have retirement savings haven't stockpiled enough to sustain them throughout their retirement.

It's never too late to start saving, though. The most important thing is to start—and, hopefully, start *big*. Your savings target should be 10 percent of your gross income. If you can do more, even better. Many plans, such as a 401(k) and various IRAs, will allow those fifty or over to make larger contributions. For example, if you're over fifty, you can put $24,000 per year pre-tax into a 401(k). That's $6,000 more than someone under fifty. You can still take advantage of compound interest. Of course, the magic ingredient— time—is less, but as long as you still have some left, make the most of it.

In addition to saving, I encourage procrastinators to take a look at their current finances and determine how much they'll need in retirement. If they discover a shortfall of savings, then I urge them to begin cutting back on expenses. Now is a good time to begin establishing better spending habits.

Deborah's Story

I was invited to a cocktail party a few years ago where I met "Deborah." As soon as Deborah learned that I was in the financial industry, she sidled up next to me and asked if she could ask a few questions about her retirement. Always eager to help a girlfriend, I told her to ask away.

Deborah had turned fifty-six a couple of weeks before the party, and she was concerned that she hadn't saved enough for retirement.

---

[48]Saad-Lessler, Joelle, Teresa Ghilarducci, and Kate Bahn. "Joelle Saad-Lessler, Teresa Ghilarducci, and Kate Bahn." Accessed May 13, 2016. http://www.economicpolicyresearch.org/images/docs/research/retirement_securi ty/Are_US_Workers_Ready_for_Retirement.pdf
[49] *Ibid*

I asked Deborah what kind of savings plans she had, and she blushed and admitted that she really wasn't sure. She said that she'd been working for the same event planning organization for almost ten years, and although she knew the business had set up a retirement plan for her, that was about all she knew.

It turned out that Deborah not only didn't know what kind of retirement plan her employer had her in, but she also had no idea what the balance was on the plan. I urged Deborah to make an appointment to see me because I had nothing to go on without this information.

A week later, Deborah came to my office. She brought her paystub, bank statements, and the most recent statement from what turned out to be an SEP IRA. After reviewing her materials, I had a much clearer picture of her situation. Although she had taken an interest in her retirement a bit late, I assured her that it was never too late to start planning.

Deborah had recently entered into a period of her financial life that was rather important, so I was glad she came to see me. Roughly around ten years before you plan to retire, or before you anticipate you'll stop working full time, is a really critical time for retirement planning. I consider this decade the "home stretch" of money-accumulating years. This is when it's crucial to have a serious conversation with a financial professional about your retirement lifestyle and the annual cost of it in the not-too-distant future.

Many people often ask how to determine the amount of money they'll need in retirement. In order to figure this out, I'll start by looking at how much a client currently spends. The next big question is to know *when* a client plans to retire.

Once I had a better idea of how much Deborah's retirement would cost, I took a look at how much she had already saved. After accounting for Deborah's estimated Social Security income, as well as for any other potential sources of post-retirement income, I could determine whether or not Deborah was in good shape financially or if she needed to increase her savings—and by how much. It turned out that Deborah's current means weren't enough to allow her to cover both her essentials and increase her retirement contributions to reach her goals before she intended to retire. Consequently, we discussed how much longer Deborah needed to keep working in order to hit her retirement savings need.

If you're in the same boat as Deborah, I urge you to seek advice from a financial professional *now*—not five years from now. You're still young enough that with a little financial planning, you can make some changes today that will have a very significant impact on both *when* you can retire and your *financial quality of life* once in retirement.

Expect the Unexpected: Rosie's Story

Sometimes you've done your planning and you're confident that you have everything all lined up for your retirement needs when— BAM!—something you never expected happens. With many companies downsizing and the job market filled with highly-skilled, very young, and extremely eager Millennials, you might find yourself unemployed before you planned to retire.

A client, "Rosie," called me the other day. Rosie was a very high-level education administrator. Not planning to retire until she was sixty-eight, Rosie found herself unemployed six years earlier than she had hoped due to her university's downsizing.

When Rosie told me of her unemployed status, I assumed that with her credentials, universities would be banging down her door in the hope of hiring her. However, after a year on unemployment, Rosie was still looking for a job. She explained that she had hired a team of professionals—head hunters, job coaches, job hunting groups—to assist with the search, but nothing had helped. During her pursuit for employment, Rosie met quite a few other top administrators and executives with similar credentials who also found themselves unemployable.

Although Rosie had the experience and expertise, universities could hire two or three lower-paid Millennials for the cost of her one enormous salary. Rosie had recently realized that she had no choice but to retire earlier than planned. As a result, her previous retirement savings, which had been based on a later retirement date, were now insufficient.

This possibility is important to bear in mind as you plan for retirement. You might assume you'll be able to work to a certain age, but the world economy might have other ideas. Be sure you consider this when working with your financial specialist.

Keep Your Options Open

Life sometimes throws us a curveball. This is why there needs to be a back-up plan for your retirement. Whether it's downsizing your lifestyle or changing your career path, it's smart to have options in the event your retirement goals aren't attainable. Besides the obvious choice—wait to retire—there are other possibilities for those who need to supplement their income or who just aren't ready to stop working.

If you find yourself in a situation like Rosie, there is always the opportunity to become an independent consultant or accept a lower-paying job with less responsibility and stress. Both of these choices provide a way to use your talents while keeping you financially on track for retirement.

These unexpected retirement blips can also offer the opportunity to consider starting your own business based on your professional skills. A friend, "Cassie," had reached retirement age but wasn't quite ready to stop working. She couldn't see herself spending her days at the beach or playing golf with her husband at the country club.

Having been an executive assistant for over thirty years, Cassie's computer and organizational skills were unmatchable. Although Cassie wasn't ready for retirement, she wanted a flexible schedule and the ability to work from home. After considerable research, she decided to start a virtual personal assistant business. Inundated with referrals, Cassie soon had more work than she had planned. Instead of turning down potential clients, Cassie began hiring other assistants. Before the end of her first year, she had hired seven virtual assistants who handled all of the clients' work while Cassie managed the company and attracted new business.

Regardless of your reason for not retiring, you should always look for the silver lining of the situation. You never know—you might end up finding gold.

Financial Questions to Ask about
Planning Your Retirement

1. Am I currently saving enough to ensure I can afford the lifestyle I want in retirement?

2. Are my investments earning compound interest?

3. What is an appropriate level of risk I should be willing to accept for my retirement savings?

4. What investments should I have in my 401(k) and other retirement accounts?

5. Should I contribute more to my retirement account(s) to reduce my taxes?

6. What should I do with my 401(k) (or other retirement account) that is with a previous employer?

7. What are some of the best ways to "catch up" if I've started saving too late?

Let's Hear from the Expert

Cory Goldman, CRPC

Cory Goldman is a Northern Illinois University graduate and has completed the CFP™ coursework through Northwestern University. In 2015 Cory obtained his CRPC® designation and became a Chartered Retirement Plan Consultant.

Plan Early for a Sunny Retirement

Every last one of us can harness an amazingly powerful force called *compound interest*! If you think of compound interest as a car, *time* is the gas you put in this vehicle. The more gas you've got, the further you can go.

The phrase "time is money" couldn't be more relevant here.

Let's look at a simplified example. We invest $100,000 today and make an average return at a reasonable rate of 8 percent. In ten years' time we now have $215,892. In *thirty* years' time however, our $100,000 is now worth a whopping $1,006,266! All we did was harness the power of compound interest fueled with *time*. Let's see how this applies if our goal coincidentally calls for $1,000,000 of savings. By starting thirty years out from retirement, we only needed to put away $100,000. However, if we had started ten years out from retirement we'd need to put away $463,193 today to reach our goal! I think we can all agree that the better method is the one that costs $363,193 less.

Achieving your picture-perfect retirement isn't a complicated business. The number one financial activity you can do for your future self is to save and invest *today*. The specific investment you choose is far less important than the time you allow for your savings to reap the benefits of compound interest.

The earlier you start, the less you need to save. Simple. Someone who makes a modest income in all of their working years can easily provide themselves with a worry-free and financially-secure retirement by starting to plan and save early. Do yourself the biggest money favor you can possibly do for yourself and make sure you have a plan in place and follow it to the letter.

Then, when the time comes, filled with pride and accomplishment, you'll be basking in your sunny retirement.

Retirement Planning for Procrastinators

Financial planning is procrastinator-friendly!

Retirement. 401(k). The market. Mutual funds. S&P 500. Interest. Taxes. If you're like most people I work with, these words don't exactly trigger feelings of excitement or action. That, coupled with the endless to-do lists most everyone's lives come with is a combination that all-too-frequently results with financial planning's demotion to the bottom of the pile. Fortunately, we live in a time where the majority of this burden can be lifted by implementing an automated retirement plan.

Setting up automatic and consistent savings is the modern day "life-hack," or rather, "retirement-hack."

By automating the retirement planning process, we benefit in two major ways. One: We're ensuring that we're saving enough! By automating this process, the correct amount that we need to save is put away before we have the chance to get our hands on the money and spend it elsewhere. This way we stay on track. Two: It's emotionally painless. No one likes to manually send money away. Even though in reality you're sending it to yourself, it still feels as if you're losing control since the cash isn't right there in your checking account.

As long as you implement an automated savings plan, you can procrastinate on your financial planning for years and still be equally (or even more so) as effective as the next guy or gal who is very mindful and attentive to their finances.

Wrap-Up

Why You Want to Start Saving Early

1. The sooner you begin putting your money into a retirement plan, the more wealth you're going to accumulate.

2. You can't afford not to invest your money!

3. Compound interest is the eighth wonder of the world. It's like a BOGO on interest.

4. Compound interest allows the investor to continuously invest the interest; simple interest does not.

5. Time is the magical ingredient in compound interest. Time allows your money to grow longer.

6. There are only three ways to increase your retirement savings—put more money away, work longer, or make your money work for you. I prefer the latter.

7. It's never too late to start saving for retirement. However, it's best to start big—10 percent of your gross income.

8. Many retirement plans—401(k), IRA, etc., will allow you to increase your contribution when you reach fifty years old. Take advantage of this!

9. The ten years before you plan to retire is the most crucial time period because you still have time to save.

10. Don't count on working to your planned retirement age. Sometimes companies downsize or go out of business, and the job market is filled with highly skilled Millennials eager to work.

Conclusion

You've Only Just Begun

T he end of this book marks the beginning of the next chapter of your life. The discussion has only begun, girlfriends, and there's a whole lot more talking to do.

As you use these guidelines to have fierce financial conversations, you should feel free to bring in a financial professional or coach. You want one who will help you understand the right questions to ask so you're not nodding your head up and down blankly.

Above all, you should get used to thinking of yourself as being in charge of your life and your money; it's your responsibility as well as your opportunity, and it's ultimately about your personal freedom to chart your course in life and take care of yourself and your loved ones.

I'm not saying that you have to be the earner in the family to take responsibility for your financial future. If you and your partner made a deal that he earns while you stay home with the kids or vice versa, your job is to make your partner accountable by keeping yourself accountable. It's on both of you to secure your financial safety for you and your family.

I firmly believe that knowledge is power, and you now have the power to initiate fierce financial conversations to help you take charge of your life and money. It's time to let the world hear you— your expression, words, views, thoughts, speeches, statements, and intuition. It's time to let the world hear your passions and commitments.

The days of needing to be likeable above all else are over! Voice your opinions and offer your perspectives. If *you* don't do it, who will? You don't want your daughters and granddaughters to remain as silent as many women have for centuries. This is your opportunity to change the future for women, and it all starts with talking about money.

I'm passing the baton to *you*! Until women begin to break the taboo of talking about money and having fierce financial conversations, they won't have equal representation in politics or in corporate America. We're in a bottleneck of having the same level of education as men, but the leadership is lacking. We need more women leaders in business and in government. This, my dear friends, is the next step in our evolution.

I realize it's not always going to be easy to step out of your comfort zone. This takes raw courage. For this reason, I invite you to stay close to the *Let's Talk about Money* movement of women who are ready to be fierce, talk straight, and not run back to the corner of the boxing ring when they've had a punch thrown at them. That was me until very recently. But now, I punch back, and it feels great. I've learned that people listen and respect you when you speak up. They don't automatically dismiss you. And most importantly, that target sign you've been wearing on your back all those years begins to disappear.

I invite you to join me online where I offer workshops, group training, and one-on-one coaching. Let's take the next step together as I guide you through finding your words and your courage and help you take risks and let your voice be heard. Help me pass the torch on to the next generation of women so they know how to speak up about money.

Girlfriends, let's keep talking!

Don't Stop Now!

What's the next step?

1. Join the conversation by signing up at:

   askjanicegoldman.com

   Here you can follow my weekly blogs, workshop announcements, teleclasses, and so much more.

2. Join the private Let's Talk about Money Facebook community where you can chat with like-minded girlfriends who will cheer you on and encourage you when you need a pep talk. This is also the place to share your past oversights with other girlfriends. The most successful people are those who have had failures or mishaps but have learned from them and offered a wake-up call so others don't make the same mistakes.

3. Follow me on Facebook at Let's Talk about Money.

4. Follow me on Twitter at @askjaniceg.

5. Join Let's Talk about Money for private and group coaching and support. Sign up at askjanicegoldman.com

6. Email me your questions and comments at:

   askjanicegoldman@gmail.com

Resources

Talk to Your Spouse about Money

American Association for Marriage and Family Therapy
http://www.aamft.org/iMIS15/AAMFT/

Prenuptial Agreement

USA. gov
https://www.usa.gov/family

Catholic Marriage Prep
http://www.catholicmarriageprep.com/

Divorce

The Lilac Tree
http://thelilactree.org/

Women's Divorce Resource Center
http://www.womens-divorce.org/

USA.gov
https://www.usa.gov/family

Parent Center
http://www.parentingcenter.com/federaldivorceandmarriage.html

Human Rights Campaign
http://www.hrc.org/resources/an-overview-of-federal-rights-and-pr
otections-granted-to-married-couples

Catholic Marriage Prep
http://www.catholicmarriageprep.com/

Association of Family and Conciliation Courts
http://www.afccnet.org/resource-center/resources-for-families/cate
goryid/1

Remarriage

Human Rights Campaign
http://www.hrc.org/resources/an-overview-of-federal-rights-and-pr
otections-granted-to-married-couples

Parenting Center
http://www.parentingcenter.com/federaldivorceandmarriage.html

Catholic Marriage Prep
http://www.catholicmarriageprep.com/

Interfaith Family
http://www.interfaithfamily.com/

Job Negotiation

USA.gov
https://www.usa.gov/jobs-and-unemployment

Salary Expert
https://www.salaryexpert.com/

Salary.com
http://www.salary.com/

Benefits and Taxes

IRS
https://www.irs.gov

Being a Financial Role Model

EveryDollar
https://www.everydollar.com

Bankrate
http://www.bankrate.com/calculators/index-of-credit-card-calculat
ors.aspx

Student Loans

Federal Student Aid: FAFSA
https://fafsa.ed.gov/

Student Loans.gov
https://studentloans.gov/myDirectLoan/index.action

Student College Board: Financial Aid PROFILE
https://student.collegeboard.org/css-financial-aid-profile

Senior Abuse

National Committee for the Prevention of Elder Abuse
http://www.preventelderabuse.org/elderabuse/fin_abuse.html

National Adult Protective Services Association
http://www.napsa-now.org/policy-advocacy/exploitation/

IRS
https://www.irs.gov/Individuals/Identity-Protection

National Committee for the Protection of Elder Abuse
http://www.preventelderabuse.org/elderabuse/fin_abuse.html

Online Dating Fraud

FBI
https://www.fbi.gov/news/stories/2012/february/dating-scams_021412

Romance Scams
http://www.romancescams.org/

FBI IC3
http://www.ic3.gov/crimeschemes.aspx

Looks Too Good to Be True
http://www.lookstoogoodtobetrue.com/stories.aspx

Estate Planning

AARP
http://www.aarp.org/money/estate-planning/

<u>American Bar Association</u>
http://www.americanbar.org/groups/real_property_trust_estate/reso
urces/estate_planning.html

<u>IRS</u>
https://www.irs.gov/Businesses/Small-Businesses-&-Self-Employe
d/Estate-and-Gift-Taxes

Retirement Planning

<u>Social Security Administration Retirement Calculators</u>
https://www.ssa.gov/planners/benefitcalculators.html

https://www.ssa.gov/retire/estimator.html

<u>AARP</u>
http://www.aarp.org/money/money-essentials/

Meet the Experts

Janice L. Boback

Janice L. Boback is a managing partner of the law firm of Anderson & Boback, a Chicago law firm which specializes in domestic relations handling such matters as divorce, custody, support, abduction, orders of protection, paternity, pre-nuptial agreements, qualified domestic relations orders, and numerous post decree matters. www.illinoislawforyou.com

Katie C. Galanes

Katie C. Galanes joined Grunyk & Associates, P.C. in October of 2013. Previously, Katie began her career at a family law firm located in downtown Chicago. While working in family law, Katie gained extensive experience in the areas of divorce, child custody, parenting time, child support, maintenance, asset valuation and allocation, and post-decree issues including college contribution and modifications of support. www.grunyklaw.com

Lora Georgieva

The founder of Destination College, Lora Georgieva is a Certified College Planner, with more than 10 years of financial planning experience. Lora graduated college with a Bachelor's degree in Actuarial Science, double major in Accounting. Her passion to start her college planning business came from her two children and from seeing many of her financial planning clients rob their retirement to pay for college. www.destination-college.org

Cory Goldman

Cory Goldman is a Northern Illinois University graduate and has completed the CFP™ coursework through Northwestern University. In 2015 Cory obtained his CRPC® designation and became a Chartered Retirement Plan Consultant. Email Cory at cgold17@gmail.com

Carolyn Kitty

Since 1982, Carolyn Kitty has provided comprehensive accounting and tax services to small business and individuals. Her clients are individuals and small businesses who appreciate personal service and don't wish to get lost in a large accounting firm. Carolyn's mission is to help her clients manage their businesses and taxes as well as avoid related problems by providing them with the benefit of her 30+ years of experience in business and accounting. www.Ckittycpa.com

Alan Pearlman

Alan Pearlman is a family law attorney who has provided legal services to Chicago and Lake County residents for over four decades. In addition, Alan is a member of several Bar Association groups and teaches both family law and legal technology. He also serves on numerous legal technology committees and was appointed by the Illinois Supreme Court to the Special Supreme Court Committee on E-Business for the State of Illinois. www.alanpearlmanltd.com

Ralph Picker

Ralph Picker, CPA & Managing Principal, has extensive experience in a wide variety of diverse business industries, with special emphasis in business audit and tax consulting for multi-operating businesses and individuals. He is experienced in all aspects of tax, accounting, audit engagements, and business consulting. Ralph has written several articles in his specialized fields of expertise and is a frequently requested speaker nationwide. He is known for his innovative approaches in his respective industries. He is a member of the American Institute of CPAs, Illinois CPA Society, and other specialized organizations. www.pickercpa.com

Kenneth H. Richman

Kenneth Richman concentrates his practice in the areas of Corporate, Labor and Employment, and Health Care law at Burke, Warren, MacKay & Serritella. For more than thirty years, he has served as general corporate counsel to privately held businesses including middle market manufacturers and distributors, start-up entities, and service providers, and he has represented business owners and their families in a broad variety of personal and business planning matters. Kenneth's experience encompasses a wide variety of commercial transactions; domestic and foreign investment and sourcing matters; and organizational, governance, succession planning, and creditor issues. www.burkelaw.com

Victoria Sushan

Victoria is a Financial Advisor, CDFA, Mediator and Collaborative Divorce Professional. She founded The Art of Living Institute, an organization offering educational resources, workshops and seminars in financial mindfulness, debt management, life coaching, stress management, divorce education and support groups and variety of classes to support, educate and empower the community. www.the-art-of-living-inc.com

Francis K. Tennant

Francis K. Tennant is partner in the firm of Wolf & Tennant and engaged in the general practice of law. He also represents units of local government and individuals in municipal law, land use and planning. He has a broad range of experience in estate planning, wills, trusts, probate and trust administration as well as business organization and representation. Francis has an extensive civil trial and appellate practice. He has tried numerous cases to verdict including personal injury, wrongful death and commercial matters, and has successfully represented his clients in the Illinois and Federal Courts. www.wolfandtennant.com

Benjamin W. Wong

Benjamin W. Wong focuses his practice on estate and business planning, real estate and estate and trust administration. Benjamin formerly worked at Deloitte and Touche, a major accounting and tax firm, and Horwood, Marcus & Berk, a mid-size downtown Chicago law firm, and at Rozman & Wong, LLC, before starting Benjamin

W. Wong & Associates, Ltd. Benjamin received both his J.D. and LL.M. in Taxation from the Chicago-Kent College of Law. He earned his B.S. from the University of Illinois at Urbana-Champaign. Ben is a frequent lecturer in the areas of business, estate planning, and real estate. www.bwwalaw.com

About Janice Goldman

Janice Goldman is a nationally recognized transformational speaker, empowerment coach, and facilitator. She regularly speaks at conferences and events throughout the United States. Her media appearances have included ABC News, Chicago Sun-Times, Chicago Fox News, DNAinfoChicago, Refinery29, and Make it Better. She has also developed a signature presentation and workshop series that includes issues surrounding the stigma of talking about money.

A survivor herself, Janice has endured numerous obstacles in her life. At the age of thirty-five, her husband passed away from leukemia while she was pregnant with twins. To her surprise, her husband's estate was not set up properly, and as a result, she was left with nothing. With twins on the way, she had no time to fall apart and mourn. Instead, she took charge of her life and built a successful career as a financial advisor and business owner. She knows firsthand the struggles of being a single woman and single mother. Recently remarried, she has also discovered the challenges and successes of blending a family.

Having developed the Women's Financial Services Division at Howe Barnes Hoefer & Arnett and worked as Senior Vice President/Vice President at such prominent financial institutions as Salomon Smith Barney, Mesirow Financial and Merrill Lynch, Janice has over thirty-two years of financial experience under her belt. She specializes in working with women who need to learn how to make the necessary choices in order to thrive in their financial and personal lives. Most of her clients are women who have survived personal setbacks such as divorce, widowhood, illness, or disability. Her mission is to help women not only survive these setbacks but to also help them embrace their financial and life goals and dreams. Janice provides her clients with a sense of balance in their work, personal, and financial lives.

Janice earned a B.A. from the University of Arizona and also has an M.A. in Arts Administration and an M.A. in Counseling and Guidance.

Acknowledgements

Writing a book like *Let's Talk About Money* can't be done alone. In addition to all of the outstanding support I received from my team during the process of writing it, I couldn't have even started if I hadn't worked with so many wonderful women throughout my thirty-two years in the financial industry. It wasn't until I discovered the joy of teaching women about their finances that I realized my passion for empowering women.

I believe that all things happen for a reason, and although the loss of my first husband was incredibly painful, his death gave me strength I never knew I had. The experience transformed me from a pampered princess into a courageous warrior.

Finding love late in life is a gift, and my gift is the bliss I've discovered with my brilliant and loving husband, Ralph Picker. Ralph, a CPA and financial expert, has stood beside me every step of the way as I made the journey from book idea to book reality. I am so grateful to live and love such a bright and supportive man.

Had it not been for my children, I might never have found my voice. As a single mom of three beautiful children, I had no choice but to speak up and fight for my kids. My business partner and son, Cory, supports me in everything I attempt. As a seasoned professional in the financial industry to women of all ages and backgrounds, he knows firsthand the importance of protecting his female clients and their families. I would be lost without Jason, my social media maven kid, who is always there to help his mom understand hashtags and tweets. My brilliant and beautiful Jahna has grown into such a strong and powerful woman that I am bursting with admiration and pride as she enters the world of computer science at the University of Chicago. I am blessed to have produced three wonderful and compassionate children.

A smart woman is never intimidated by power and strength. She wants to have the best people possible on her team. It's no accident that Elba Patzelt is at the top of my team roster. Elba is so much more than my assistant. She is my friend, my Sister in Strength, my right hand that always has a finger on my pulse, often articulating what I want to say better than I could express it. Celebrity stylist, Keith Ward, makes me feel more beautiful than I could have ever imagined. His talent goes beyond making the people in his world stunning; his mission is to help as many people as he can with his exquisite talent. I am forever grateful to him for his loving support and kindness. I knew when I first met my editor, Lynn Abbott-McCloud, that we were kindred spirits. Her clarity and insight were tremendously helpful in communicating my story. Having wanted to write this book for several years, I knew that with Lynn on the team, a die-hard runner who trains for marathons, there was no doubt we'd make it to the finish line. And my final team member is my dream publisher, Maurice Bassett. Maurice is another kindred spirit who is so accomplished and such a genius that I'm truly humbled and honored to be his colleague. I couldn't imagine working with a more supportive, eager, and caring publisher.

When I contacted experts to contribute to this book, I was blown away by the excited responses. I give great thanks to the book's contributing professionals who were interested in creating a new paradigm for women. Many thanks to: Katie C. Galanes, Janice L. Bobeck, Victoria Sushan, Alan Pearlman, Ken Richman, Carolyn Kitty, Lora Georgieva, Francis K. Tennant, Benjamin W. Wong, and Cory Goldman. They are committed to empowering and educating female consumers. I also give thanks to Adri Miller-Heckman for being there to hand out the keys to the ladies' room and for always showing me the way. I would be remiss if I failed to mention some of the women who have inspired and motivated me. Barbara Stanny, Kate Northrup, and Katana Abbott have all been shining beacons guiding me toward my dreams. And of course, I want to thank my beloved canine children, Eenie and Ruby. They helped me so much with this book that they became inspired to write their own book. Watch for it later this year.

Finally, I thank all the dear, kind, and honest women who spoke up and shared in this book in order to make this world a better place for future generations of women. They desperately want a fairer and better shake for their daughters of the next generation. May their voices be heard.

Thank you for reading this book. It has been the mission of my life.

Index

Made in the USA
San Bernardino, CA
18 June 2016